"Each version of the internet brings uncertainty and opportunity. Some cling to fear, and hide. Outliers take action and create. Kary Oberbrunner and Lee Richter provide a clear path for leveraging these new emerging capabilities and confidently taking action."

—Dan Sullivan, Co-Founder and President of Strategic Coach®

"Kary Oberbrunner always seems to be out in front of cultural issues and he finds ways to help teams better themselves as he communicates his insight and foresight. Blockchain Life is a vivid example of this reality. I found myself reading it and saying, 'Yes, this is where we are going; this is how it should be done.' New days and new ways are on the horizon—and this book will equip you to be ready to seize those days."

—Dr. Tim Elmore, Founder and CEO of Growing Leaders and author of A New Kind of Diversity

"What may feel like a daunting, new world, ends up feeling like a familiar and comfortable place as Kary and Lee gracefully and easily break down a seemingly complex web of systems into an approachable portal into the future. Leveraging and entering into this new era has never felt so easy."

—Gisele Wyne, VP of Operations, GeniusX, Inc.

Governance is an essential component within all human relationships. The metaverse is no exception. Kary and Lee help us imagine this brand new Web3 world and how proper governance will help move forward into exciting opportunities and challenges.

—Debra Brown, CEO Governance Solutions, author of 4 bestselling books

"The emergence of new technologies naturally spawns the best and the worst aspects of humanity. Kary and Lee give insights on how the Web, VR/AR, and blockchain can be navigated for positive and uplifting use cases. Blockchain Life is not a technically heavy book and is accessible to anyone looking to understand these topics in more detail."

—Nick Janicki, CEO & Co-Founder, GeniusX, Inc

"Web3 and Blockchain will affect nearly every business. We can either prepare for the future now and leverage the technology or choose ignorance and miss an opportunity. In brilliant fashion, Kary and Lee show us the benefits and challenges in a clear, concise, and direct manner."

—Justin Donald, #1 National Best Selling Author and Founder of The Lifestyle Investor, Host of The Lifestyle Investor Podcast

The shift in the Internet is a natural evolution of continually creating more value. Digital currencies are a much more efficient way of exchanging value and will be the standard some day. NFT's are a much more efficient way of holding and transferring ownership titles and will be the standard some day. Kary and Lee do a great job of laying out the basics that will lead to a broader understanding, adoption, and leveraging of the blockchain.

—**Lee Benson, CEO Execute to Win,**
***WSJ* and *USA Today* bestselling author of**
Your Most Important Number

BLOCKCHAIN
LIFE

Wall Street Journal, USA Today, and Amazon International Bestselling Authors

BLOCKCHAIN LIFE

MAKING SENSE OF THE METAVERSE, NFTS, CRYPTOCURRENCY, VIRTUAL REALITY, AUGMENTED REALITY, AND WEB3

KARY OBERBRUNNER
LEE RICHTER

ethos
collective

Printed in the United States of America

Published by Ethos Collective™
PO Box 43, Powell, OH 43065
www.ethoscollective.vip

LCCN: 2022916222
Paperback ISBN: 978-1-63680-089-9
Hardcover ISBN: 978-1-63680-090-5
e-book ISBN: 978-1-63680-091-2

Available in paperback, hardcover, e-book, and audiobook

Any Internet addresses (websites, blogs, etc.) and telephone numbers
printed in this book are offered as a resource. They are not intended in
any way to be or imply an endorsement by Ethos Collective™, nor does
Ethos Collective™ vouch for the content of these sites and numbers for
the life of this book.

Some names and identifying details have been changed
to protect the privacy of individuals.

For special bonus content associated with this book including videos, trainings, and the FREE Web Quotient (WQ) assessment, visit:

TheBlockchainLife.io

Also by Kary Oberbrunner:

DEDICATION

Dan Sullivan

For connecting us together and for the many insights you imparted to us within Strategic Coach® including the concept of Free Zones™.

TABLE OF CONTENTS

Part 3: Creation 125

NOTE

I have a confession.

Regarding Web3, what's often called the new version of the internet, this book is limited and incomplete. Every single day, new updates, breakthroughs, and capabilities emerge. This is what makes this topic so exciting.

It's impossible to provide a solution for every question. Many competent experts have come before and many more will come after.

Rather than providing exhaustive answers, the purpose of this book was born out of my desire to help friends, families, and clients get clarity. We all sense the changes coming. Most of us just don't have the time or ability to dive deep. We want to stay relevant, but we don't have the bandwidth to discern between hype and hope.

And so this book serves as a primer in achieving that goal.

Now, about the length. In the spirit of Blaise Pascal's quote—"I would have written a shorter letter, but I did not have the time"—I'm making this book as short as possible.

Longer is easier. Shorter is better.

Perfection is not my goal either. That's an impossible one and a standard that causes the strongest author to suffer writer's block.

Therefore, inspired by Antoine de Saint-Exupery, I've removed every "filler" word. I anchored his quote in my mind:

"Perfection is achieved, not when there is nothing more to add, but when there is nothing left to take away."

After mountains of research, my filter transitioned from—what can I add? To—**what can I not take away?**

And finally, my last note, this one about my co-author, Lee Richter.

I started my new business Blockchain Life about six months before reaching out to her for the first time. I heard about her and her wisdom regarding NFTs specifically. We run in similar circles,

Strategic Coach™ being one of them. I found her on social media and started following her. Immediately, I resonated with her depth and breadth on the topic.

I sent her a DM and asked if we could chat about potentially co- authoring a book on blockchain. I knew there was much to learn on this topic, and I knew Lee could sharpen me.

We've enjoyed a kindred spirit connection. Fast forward nine months, and our shared passion has taken us across the world and back. (She made it as far as Antarctica!)

Co-authoring can be tricky. Oftentimes, the authors get in the way of their readers.

Who's talking now?
Kary the man or Lee the woman?

And to make it more complex, our names are shared by multiple genders.

Kary can be a woman's name.

Lee can be a man's name.

Inserting pronouns in the book would be super confusing.

So, to save you sideways energy, and to put you first, I'll write the book in first person.

When appropriate, I'll reference my amazing thinking partner, Lee. In the writing process, she supplied me with articles, blogs, reports, and white papers. I am forever grateful.

Oh, and if you're worried about us pushing an agenda, rest easy. We're not selling anything.

We've been through crypto bull markets and crypto bear markets. I'm in my forties. Lee is in her fifties. We're both owners of multiple businesses. We have international teams, and we create products and services.

My point?

We're not into fads, trends, or getting-rich-quick schemes. Rather, we're genuinely interested in the new capabilities made possible by emerging Web3 technology. We believe it can and will shape every fabric of our lives. For this reason, it's our duty to prepare you so you can leverage new opportunities. What you do with this knowledge is completely up to you.

Now with all that behind us, let's unpack how we arrived here—the most exciting time in human history.

PART 1
CONTEXT

INTERNET

Exercise Mom

A fifty-year-old wife and mother straps on a virtual reality headset in her quiet suburban house. As someone who's struggled with weight her entire life, she's given up on exercise—believing she's just not "one of those people."

Doctors warn her yet again about the serious health challenges confronting her if she continues to ignore their pleas. Fitness clubs feel intimidating, and sweaty yoga classes with strangers make her feel anxious.

In the privacy of her living room, she can access a wide array of activities:

Battle fire-breathing dragons.

Hang glide over sun-scorched mountains. Swim in azure, shark-infested oceans.

Scale sharp, death-defying walls.

The best news?

She's making healthy choices for the first time in a long time. Her weight is down. And her endorphins are up. She's now in control of her future, and she feels unstoppable.

Preteen Artist

A twelve-year-old girl draws in her bedroom late one evening. The city is alive with action right outside her window. After a short while, another long-necked lady emerges on her canvas. Her masterpiece isn't for an art class at school but rather a piece in her NFT collection that has earned well over $5 million dollars in profits, not to mention even more in secondary sales.

Time Magazine, her latest customer, commissioned her next creation. She'll have to start turning down clients as her calendar nears capacity from a slew of paid speaking gigs booked at technology conferences all over the world.[1]

Metaverse Church

A mega-church based in Oklahoma already ministers to hundreds of thousands of people at multiple campuses in multiple countries. In the past few months, they've added yet another church service—this one, in the metaverse. During the very first service, three people gave their lives to Jesus Christ.[2]

What started out as an experiment with a single church sparked an immersive movement across many denominations. Metaverse churches are popping up all over virtual lands—staffed with greeters, musicians, and preachers. Visitors can even tithe in cryptocurrencies if they want to invest in the ministry and spread the Gospel.

Evidently, they believe Jesus' Great Commission—God into all the world—even includes digital worlds like the metaverse.

Constitution DAO

When one of the last remaining copies of the United States Constitution went up for sale back in 2021, a group of online enthusiasts talked about pooling their money together to buy it.

Although it seemed improbable, in five days, they raised $47 million in cryptocurrency. In the end, their campaign was unsuccessful when billionaire Ken Griffin purchased the historic document at a Sotheby's auction.[3]

Nonetheless, this eclectic group made a profound statement about the power and potential of decentralized autonomous organizations (DAOs), the new governing entity of choice for many Web3 projects.

A Brave New (Digital) World?

These four stories only scratch the surface of what's possible with Web3. The new world we find ourselves in has no boundaries, no borders, and hardly any rules. It's reshaping the way we do life and business, and just like the explorers of old, many pioneers are venturing into the vast unknown.

Crypto.com capitalized (pun intended) on this metaphor in its 2022 Super Bowl commercial showcasing explorers throughout history.

The infamous advertisement concluded with a sharp exhortation, "Fortune favors the brave."[4]

Turns out we no longer have a choice. Aldous Huxley's Brave New World is upon us, ready or not.

This book forged out of a deep conviction that we're truly not in Kansas anymore. Maybe a metaverse digital twin of Kansas but definitely not the familiar one.

Pushing The Wizard of Oz metaphor a little further, here's the truth. There's a new wizard, there's a new Oz, and the stakes in this new universe are much higher. Forget your ruby slippers. The way this story ends could reshape humanity as a species.

How? you might ask. This yellow brick road promises a new reality, with a new currency, new assets, and maybe even a new transhuman species.

In our journey, you'll confront innovation on a new level. You think the world was wild before? Strap on your VR goggles. You're about to encounter:

- Humans having sex with robots
- Investors spending millions on digital images of apes and rocks
- People buying virtual real estate
- Teenagers spending a fortune on luxury goods they'll never touch

Although some might see a land of golden opportunities, others see a dangerous hell of unspeakable evil. In its relatively short existence, metaverse visitors experienced:

- Virtual Nazi concentration camp digital reenactments
- Strip clubs where kids' avatars are invited to get naked and perform sex acts
- Bullying and hate crimes committed in virtual worlds by virtual characters
- Breach of data, property, and security

Reality has been redefined and—referencing the Web3 illustrations above—new questions emerge with our four examples:

Exercise Mom: Do calories burned in the virtual world also count in the real world? Is exercising with VR goggles strapped to your head hazardous to your health—albeit mental or emotional health?

Preteen Artist: Should a preteen be entrusted with millions of dollars? How are NFTs even taxed anyway?

Metaverse Church: Is the metaverse the Devil's new playground, and a virtual one at that? Do extramarital affairs in virtual worlds still count as adultery in the real world?

Constitution DAO: How do you divide a historical document among hundreds of strangers? Who's ultimately liable within DAOs?

Whether we like it or not, we're caught in Web3, where governance is up for grabs.[5] Before we decide where to go from here, it's wise to discover how we got here in the first place. Doing so gives us context for this digital puzzle—a puzzle worth solving.

Web1, Web2, Web3

Model Ts aren't the same as Lamborghinis.

(For starters, Model Ts don't have gas pedals.)

You can still drive a Model T, but the world is no longer equipped to support them. Service stations aren't. Roads aren't. Other drivers aren't.

Notice the similarities when our illustration moves from cars to the Internet.

Web1 isn't the same as Web3.

(For starters, Web1 meant you couldn't use the landline phone while using the Internet.)

You can still use Web1, but the world is no longer equipped to support it. Websites aren't. Banks aren't. Other businesses aren't.

You get the point. Just because Web1 or Web2 still exists doesn't mean it's efficient or effective. Given a matter of time, this technology will become obsolete and perhaps in some cases even dangerous.

(Imagine running a nuclear power plant or even the local emergency room at the hospital on Web1.)

Although exact dates vary, the three versions of the Internet are often categorized as follows:

Web1 = 1991–2004
Web2 = 2004–2021
Web3 = 2022–?

Some haters deny the existence of Web3, evidenced by Elon Musk's tweet on December 21, 2021:

"Has anyone seen web3? I can't find it."

Although Musk is often perceived as a futurist, even the biggest believers have moments of doubt. Throughout history, technology has always attracted skeptics and critics. One Twitter follower (@ iamDCinvestor) felt the need to remind Musk how resistance is futile.

"Has anyone seen the Internet? I can't find it."—someone in 1992 who didn'tbelieve the Internet existed.

Ouch!

But Musk is not alone in his dissent for Web3. Former Twitter CEO Jack Dorsey said, "Web3 idea is not a force for democratizing the web, but instead a tool of the venture capitalists."[6]

Another critic posted his thoughts in the comment section of an article. "It's pretty easy to distill Web3. It's hype, lies and scams."[7]

Why include criticism about Web3 in a book on Web3? Aren't I trying to convince you of the validity and superiority of Web3?

Nope.

The good news is we don't need to convince you of anything. Our job is simply to present the facts. Besides, we want you to understand that criticism is alive and well. Denying it only erodes your trust. As your guides, we're committed to presenting the whole picture. Then you'll need to make your own choice.

Regardless of your belief or unbelief of Web3, no one can argue the Internet today is very different from back in 1991. For those of us alive in the 90s, get ready to experience a little nostalgia.

Whether or not you were alive, the following Web Comparison Chart™ demonstrates these differences:

Bonus Video

Web Comparison Chart™

©2022 Kary Oberbrunner. Permission granted to use with attribution anywhere, everywhere.

	Web 1 1991-2004	**Web 2** 2004-2021	**Web 3** 2022-?
Motto	*They create.* *They own.*	*We create.* *They own.*	*We create.* *We own.*
Access	Desktop	Mobile	Wearable
Assets	Physical	Digital	NFTs
Benefit	Informational	Social	Experiential
Byproduct	Information Gathering	Data Mining	Open Source
Component	Advertising	Algorithms	Artificial Intelligence
Control	Decentralized	Centralized	Decentralized
Currency	Credit Cards	Payment Aggregators	Cryptocurrencies
Danger	Phishing	Hacking	Deepfaking
Economy	Information	Attention	Creator
Experience	Static	Dynamic	Interactive
Extreme	Dot-Com Bubble	*The Social Dilemma*	Transhumanism
Function	Reading	Writing	Executing
Governance	Individuals	Big Tech	DAOs
Image	Clip Art	Videos	Gaming Engines
Intellectual Property	Copyright / Trademark Patent	Digital Signature	Easy IP™
Legal	Physical Contract	Digital Contract	Smart Contract
Login	Username / Password	Social	Web3 Wallet
Reality	Physical Reality	Augmented Reality	Mixed Reality
Technology	No Blockchain	Private Blockchain	Public Blockchain
Venue	Sites	Platforms	Metaverses

Perhaps the chart feels overwhelming or maybe exciting. In the beginning probably both. Desmond TuTu told us how to eat this proverbial elephant—one bite at a time.[8] And that's exactly how we laid out the book.

- Part One is intentionally brief. Our goal was simply to show you the existence of different versions of the Internet.

- Part Two, things will get exciting. You'll understand how everything is shifting. We're privileged to be the generation to see it and shape it. We'll unpack these components one at a time and how each is expressed in Web1, Web2, and Web3.

- Part Three, we'll end with a practical appeal. You'll have the opportunity to decide how you want to show up in Web3: as a critic, a consumer, or a creator?

Get ready. A brand new world awaits.

PART 2
COMPARISON

MOTTO

	Web 1 1991-2004	Web 2 2004-2021	Web 3 2022- ?
Motto	**They Create. They Own.**	**We Create. They Own.**	We create. We own.

Hopefully, the first word children usually speak is mama or dada. However, in no time at all, another word pops into their vocabulary.

MINE!

Scan the planet, and you'll see how every creature considers ownership a primal right. Whether it's lions and a fresh kill, squirrels and a jackpot of acorns, or humans and a folder of intellectual property, something deep inside elevates ownership as a top physical, emotional, and social need.

This is where we'll start, with the mottos surrounding ownership.

Web 1: They Create. They Own.

Take a pizza joint back in Web1. If that restaurant wanted to flex and stake a claim on the World Wide Web, it might have uploaded its menu online.

Doing so bypassed the yellow pages. For those unaware of the yellow pages, imagine a five-inch thick dictionary-looking book issued a couple of times a year.

If you had a craving, you looked under P for pizzas in the big thick book. Once you found the right section, you poured over the pages, scouring for the one with the best ad.

Next, you made a phone call on a landline or used twenty-five cents to call from a pay phone. When your call finally went through, you asked the person on the other line to read you the menu. Eventually, after some back-and-forth discussion, you placed the order and then picked up the pizza. (Deliveries were few and far between before the days of DoorDash.)

They created the website, and they owned it.

Businesses provided products and services, and we purchased them. Back then, we didn't even comment. They spoke, and we listened, not the picture of healthy communication. Something had to change—and it did.

Web2: We Create. They Own.

With the rise of social media, the two-way conversation began. Because we could post comments, videos, and reviews, savvy businesses listened.

Web2 measured engagement with eyeballs and eardrums, and the one with the most attention won.

Take a car company, for example. They invited us to post pictures and videos of our experience with their car. We became their "boots on the ground" marketing team who worked for free. We created the content. But they owned our content.

Many influencers found out the hard way. They built up their followers and fans on platforms owned by Big Tech. Overnight, they were muted because of changes with the "algorithm." Or worse yet, censored due to views different from the platform.

In Web2, we discovered who truly pulled the strings—and it wasn't us. We might have created the content, but we didn't own it.

Web3: We Create. We Own.

We smelled the setup and rebelled.

Some of us left social media altogether. Others made backups of our backups. We created our own platforms and gave our communities the opportunity to opt-in—bypassing corporate giants.

We stopped waiting to be picked. Instead, we picked ourselves and created our brands and businesses. We changed the game and evened the playing field.

We became the buyers, and they started knocking on our doors. Web3 humbles the proud and elevates the prepared.

We could finally compete against big budgets and deep pockets. Crowd-funding, customer reviews, and grassroots campaigns proved to be powerful weapons.

The revolution began.

Bonus Video

ACCESS

	Web 1 1991-2004	Web 2 2004-2021	Web 3 2022- ?
Access	**Desktop**	**Mobile**	**Wearable**

Back in 1999, life was much simpler. We controlled the Internet. It didn't control us.

Later that year, the first Matrix movie was released, causing quite a stir. The producers portrayed a very different future—including a future Internet. Neo accessed the Internet by sticking a long metal probe into the back of his brain.

The result was an embodied Internet, learning Kung Fu inside a simulated dojo where he felt the punches and kicks.

Embodied Internet? We've heard this storyline somewhere else:

- The next platform will be even more immersive—an embodied Internet where you're in the experience, not just looking at it. We call this the metaverse, and it will touch every product we build.

- The defining quality of the metaverse will be a feeling of presence—like you are right there with another person or in another place. Feeling truly present with another person is the ultimate dream of social technology. That is why we are focused on building this.

- In the metaverse, you'll be able to do almost anything you can imagine—get together with friends and family, work, learn, play, shop, create—as well as completely new experiences that don't really fit how we think about computers or phones today.[9]

Oh, wait.

That's not a movie. And it's not science fiction either. That was an excerpt from the Facebook Founder's Letter. Mark Zuckerberg uttered these words on October 21, 2021, the day he announced the name change to Meta.

Decked out in haptic suits, just like Neo, we can now feel punches and kicks inside this new Internet.

Web 1: Desktop

Accessing the Internet via desktop ensured clear divisions between work and play. Back in Web1, the Internet required a dial-up connection to a landline.

Since the Internet wasn't portable or mobile, if we wanted to be online, we stayed tethered to our homes or offices. These rigid guidelines ensured a compartmentalized experience. We were either online or offline—but not both.

Web2: Mobile

Everything changed with mobile. People started feeling they were always online. Digital and physical worlds merged.

Social media gave us posting power, first with status updates, then pictures, and videos. Friends and families experienced a 360-degree view of our lives, including the biggest and smallest parts.

Our existence across multiple platforms created a phenomenon called digiphrenia. Coined by Douglas Rushkoff in his book, Present Shock, digiphrenia is the result of trying to manage multiple versions of ourselves simultaneously, making it more difficult for our minds to process the digital multi-tasking.[10]

We experienced increasing anxiety produced by the instantaneous nature of digital technology. This ever-increasing speed and immediacy of time pushed us to exist on multiple platforms (email, social media, texting, phone) while remaining current, congruent, and responsive. The social pressure produced high levels of cortisol, unknown to previous generations.

Of course it was a tradeoff.

Mobile Internet created incredible efficiencies too. We could navigate any road thanks to the GPS on our phones. Mobile banking, shopping, emailing, and fitness upgraded our abilities too. Unfortunately, we didn't ask the price for remaining perpetually online.

Web3: Wearable

Back in 2014, when I wrote my dystopian novel Elixir Project, ingestibles, injectables, and implantables felt slightly out of reach.

Today, it's right in front of us. Nanotechnology is alive and well and many people's lives and health depend upon it.

Wearables went mainstream. While typing on my keyboard right now, I'm sporting two wearables: my smart watch and my smart ring.

One tracks my heartbeat, steps, miles, and numerous other metrics. The other serves as my personal sleep coach ensuring proper daily rest. Both aid me in achieving the high-performance lifestyle I crave.

Again. Trade-offs.

Each holiday season, new models of wearable technology like virtual reality goggles and augmented reality goggles are released into the market. No longer limited to gaming devices, these wearables are now found within universities, militaries, businesses, and hospitals.

We don't surf the Internet like we did back in Web1. Today, in Web3, we ask the Internet to transport us into other worlds so we can learn concepts, build companies, practice surgeries, train for war, and meet with co-workers.

Bonus Video

ASSETS

	Web 1 1991-2004	Web 2 2004-2021	Web 3 2022- ?
Assets	**Physical**	**Digital**	**NFTs**

Today, many of us earn "stars" when we frequent our local Starbucks. Earn enough, and you can redeem them for a free drink, all via the convenience of the app on your phone or watch.

I prefer earning points at Smoothie King™. I've reached "Champion" status, enabling me early access to their newest concoctions. I can order my drink via the app and skip the line when I arrive. When I pull up, the servers have my smoothie already made, chilled, and with my name on the cup—literally.

Talk about a tasty asset.

Web 1: Physical

Back in the nineties, our assets came in paper form:

- Diplomas
- Titles
- Mortgages
- Certificates
- Deeds
- Receipts
- Photographs

We liked our paper, so we bought filing cabinets to organize those papers. Then we stored those cabinets in basements and crawl spaces. When we acquired too many cabinets, we relocated them to rental storage facilities.

No wonder why we went digital.

Web2: Digital

Digital saved us time, money, and space.

Our photographs could be viewed immediately on devices. We could edit these photographs and send them to our friends in seconds. Or we could post them publicly for all the world to see.

Some of us remember the days before digital photos.

We did this weird ritual where we dropped off film at a store or pharmacy. We exercised faith, believing the store wouldn't lose or misuse our film. We hoped they'd develop our film into physical photographs.

We'd check a box if we wanted single prints or double prints. It was all a guess, anyway, because we didn't know what they looked like ahead of time.

We'd wait a while—as in days—and then we'd head back to the store to pick them up. The salesperson handed us large packs of sealed envelopes with some kind of gummy adhesive. We'd leaf through those photos, skipping the blurry ones.

Talk about expensive, inefficient, and ineffective.

This is one small example of why we transitioned our assets from paper to digital. But this transition included much more than photographs. I now receive assets in the form of digital documents from my doctor, my financial advisor, my lawyer, my CPA, my church, my alma mater, and even my government.

Web3: NFTs

Most people gloss over NFTs (non-fungible tokens), assuming they're simply digital pictures of apes. Although this is a use case, sadly it's the one that seems to get the most media coverage.

If you don't "get" NFTs, you're not alone. Most people can't make sense of the hype. My friend Tyler explained it to me back in March of 2021.

"Think of it as digital art," he said. I still didn't get it.

"Okay. Let me try another angle," Tyler said. "Do you play video games?"

"Nope."

"Do your kids?"

"Absolutely," I said. "My son plays Fortnite." "Perfect," he replied. "Has he ever bought a skin?"

My eyes lit up. I could see where he was going. My wife helped me understand the purpose of a skin several years prior. Think of it as an outfit for your character that symbolizes achievements in the game and therefore status. Other players notice your skin. It's a modern-day digital flex.

Before some of us label the next generation as ridiculous or shallow, hang on. We've been "flexing" since the first day in human history.

People wore certain shells, feathers, stones, or arrowheads. Over time, flexing transitioned to special fabrics, weapons, or hats. Maybe in your day, flexing meant wearing certain shoes or watches or perhaps attending a certain university.

The point is we've always been influenced by flexing. These days, it's just digital. And why wouldn't it be?

In my day, people "pulled up" to parties with certain vehicles. This garnered gasps from the crowd. Mission accomplished. Social currency gained.

With COVID, there were no parties. The younger generation "pulled up" to online gatherings, not in vehicles but in skins.

Same result. Mission accomplished. Social currency gained.

Although skins are digital assets, at the time of this writing, they're still not NFTs. There's a huge difference between the two.

Digital assets are a dime a dozen. You can't prove ownership, authenticity, or provenance—a big fancy word meaning, "record of ownership of a work of art or an antique."[11] Without these components, there's no scarcity and therefore little value.

It's the difference between possessing a picture of a ticket to your favorite pro sports team and possessing an actual ticket. The real ticket retains value because it's authentic and contains benefits like the ability to gain admission to an event. The real ticket represents an actual seat in an actual row in an actual section in an actual stadium. The ticket could be resold for real money and enjoyed by the new owner.

On the other hand, the picture of the ticket may look real, but it lacks authenticity, and so it lacks value. There is no game, no seat, and no ability to resell the ticket.

Before blockchain technology, digital assets didn't hold much value.

JPEGs could be passed from digital device to digital device, similar to emailing a document. Copies of digital documents don't contain value because they're not scarce.

However, once a digital asset is minted to the blockchain, a smart contract is simultaneously created. This code verifies ownership, authenticity, and provenance—proving there's only one in existence. As we'll explore later, blockchain technology also prevents alteration of the smart contract.

Besides ownership, smart contracts may contain many other benefits that can be upheld in a court of law. Some of these benefits might include perpetual royalties each time the NFT is resold.

Or perhaps the NFT unlocks off-chain benefits like access to an influencer or celebrity. NFTs can even include admission to events and experiences.

This is only the beginning.

Some NFTs are tied to bands or movies and positioned as a form of stock. The value of that NFT increases or decreases based on the future success of that band or movie.

Other NFTs represent fractionalized real estate or fine art, allowing for multiple owners, similar to the Constitution DAO mentioned at the beginning of this book.

NFTs can represent:

- Authors' books

- Musicians' songs

- Athletes' names, images, and likenesses (NIL)

Time doesn't permit us to share everything about NFTs. Besides, new use cases emerge every day. If you'd like more on this topic, visit TheBlockchainLife.io or scan the QR Code below:

We're already experiencing a seismic shift in how NFTs affect the academy, evidenced in many institutions—some in the US and some around the world:

The University of Georgia's New Media Institute was among the first to offer degrees as NFTs, as well as the option of keeping a paper certificate. They cited the benefits for students able to share their verified qualifications digitally with future employers, as well as minimizing environmental impact.[12]

Hoseo, a South Korean University, gave all 2,830 graduates of the class of 2021 a non-fungible token (NFT) degree and certificate.

Switching from paper-based diplomas to NFTs made administrative services more accessible, allowed for certificate revisions, and prevented fraud.[13]

Diplomas and degrees aren't the only use case for NFTs in the academy. NFTs are changing the way universities approach philanthropy.

The University of California, Berkeley, has used NFTs to sell pioneering research as a fundraising stream. It auctioned the patented disclosures through an NFT of Nobel

Prize-winning cancer immunotherapy research by James Allison last year, making the institution $50,000 to fund further research.[14]

Next time people try reducing NFTs into digital pictures, you can educate them (kindly) on their limited thinking. When you do, you'll expand their minds about the abundance of uses. Most likely, you'll come up with other creative uses unique to your context or industry.

That's the beauty of Web3. It's open source and decentralized. This collaborative conversation is always expanding deeper and wider.

No one will ever be able to put the "Web3 genie" back into the bottle. This genie is gaining followers by the minute, in multiple metaverses, and growing stronger by the hour.

Bonus Video

BENEFIT

	Web 1 1991-2004	Web 2 2004-2021	Web 3 2022- ?
Benefit	Informational	Social	Experiential

Start with Why.

Wise words from bestselling author, Simon Sinek. On point, it's probably a good idea to unpack why we even use the Internet in the first place. To discover the benefits, we must go back to the beginning.

Web 1: Informational

Ever since 1597, when Francis Bacon penned the phrase in his Meditationes Sacrae, we've believed Knowledge Is Power.

A quick review of history proves this, revealing how the superpowers of antiquity owned information in the form of libraries. "The world's oldest known library, The Library of Ashurbanipal, was founded sometime in the 7th century B.C. for the 'royal contemplation' of the Assyrian ruler. Located in Nineveh in modern-day Iraq, the site included a trove of some 30,000 cuneiform tablets organized according to subject matter."[15]

According to History.com, seven other ancient libraries were also noteworthy:

1. The Library of Alexandria

2. The Library of Pergamum

3. The Villa of the Papyri

4. The Libraries of Trajan's Forum

5. The Library of Celsus

6. The Imperial Library of Constantinople

7. The House of Wisdom

It's easy to test Francis Bacon's premise: Knowledge Is Power. Look no further than what attacking countries did with the libraries when they conquered them.

Did they ignore the books or do something else with the books? The attack of The House of Wisdom in Baghdad closes the loop.

This ancient masterpiece stood as the Islamic world's intellectual nerve center for several hundred years. Then, in 1258, it met a grisly end when the Mongols sacked Baghdad. According to legend, they tossed so many books into the River Tigris that the waters turned black from ink.

The Mongols knew destroying the library would deliver a death blow and wound Baghdad for centuries to come.

Although I wasn't alive in 1258, I'm old enough to remember some of the pre-Web1 Encyclopedia Britannica ads. For those unfamiliar with this company, their large set of books contained dated information on various subjects.

Their marketing messages leveraged felt needs about information and knowledge. Such headlines included:

- Give your family the greatest knowledge book of all times

- The book of knowledge

- What's important to young people is important to our people

Their angle was simple. If you care about your family and your legacy, equip them with knowledge in the form of an encyclopedia because knowledge is power.

You can see why Web1 became so powerful. Imagine all the information in the world connected with hyperlinks and the ability to be updated in real time. Rather than visiting warehouses full of books, you could now access this information at the convenience of your desktop computer.

Web2: Social

The first layer of the Internet gave us the ability to access information of every kind. The second layer of the Internet gave us the ability to access people of every kind. These two layers, combined with mobile computing, turned our worlds upside down.

Social currency became a thing because our visible network contributed to our visible net worth, at least in terms of perception. Blue check marks and verified accounts raised our social status.

Before doing business with people, we could do research on people and use that insight to work in our favor. Trust could be established before ever speaking one word.

Online dating increased, and over time, the stigma decreased. Through Web2, people found their mate, their employer, their counselor, and their doctor.

Online shopping exploded, and verified customer reviews made the process easier than ever. Businesses got smarter and integrated social networks with customer reviews, making the process informative and social. Some online stores even gave reviewers special status for the amount of reviews they completed.

The number of social platforms steadily increased, scaling quickly by allowing us to import our contacts. We willingly supplied the platforms with personal data points about everything, including our location, our likes, and our dislikes.

Web3: Experiential

In Web3, we added another layer to informational and social. We also integrated experiences.

People want experiences. Look no further than Disneyland and Universal Studios. We're also willing to pay a premium for them. Cruise ships and deep sea diving offer acceptable forms of dissociation. Dinner-themed restaurants like Medieval Times or far-off adventures like SpaceX's civilian space flights demonstrate our desire to be transported to other worlds.

This craving isn't new.

Some ancient people groups leveraged drug-induced trips to escape their woes of daily life. Today, other people choose Burning Man. Or we can skip the high and choose less dramatic examples of escapism by visiting local movie theaters or riding bicycles.

But what if we could save money, travel, and hangovers? The embodied Internet makes this possible. Our imagination is our only limitation.

Now we can go anywhere with anyone at any time.

Want to time travel back to the prehistoric age and ride a dinosaur with your deceased family member?

Want to see the miracles of Jesus with the twelve disciples and your childhood friend?

Want to live out your sexual fantasies with a celebrity crush?

All of these experiences—and more—can be yours by simply strapping on a headset.

We've entered a new era where technology has outpaced our ethics. It's a new package, wrapped around an age-old dilemma. What can we do versus what should we do?

We've evolved to a state where we choose our futures and create our worlds. In past generations, this superpower would have signified god-like status. Today, it's simply reality.

Bonus Video

BYPRODUCT

	Web 1 1991-2004	Web 2 2004-2021	Web 3 2022- ?
Byproduct	Information Gathering	Data Mining	Open Source

Now that we discovered the "why" behind the Internet by examining the benefits, it's a good idea to discover the "what" behind the Internet by examining the byproducts.

As you might assume, each version of the Internet produced different byproducts.

Web 1: Information Gathering

Prior to Web1, most people found information through traditional media sources. When Web1 arrived on the scene, the famed hyperlink connected many of these sources together.

According to "a short history of the internet," an online article by Science and Media Museum:

Tim Berners-Lee first proposed the idea of a "web of information" in 1989. It relied on "hyperlinks" to connect documents together.

Written in Hypertext Markup Language (HTML), a hyperlink can point to any other HTML page or file that sits on top of the internet.[16]

Hyperlinks allowed us to go from independent articles, searches, and entries, to an endless rabbit hole of information. Although it might sound a little "woo woo," think of this as an evolution from an independent mind to a collective consciousness. Web1 moved us closer to hive thinking.

Web2: Data Mining

Imagine people willingly sharing their most intimate thoughts, preferences, locations, memories, relationships, buying patterns, and habits for free.

It gets more interesting.

The platforms we use are designed to be addictive in nature. All our data gets tracked and processed by businesses so they can turn around and create ads that influence our behavior and manipulate us to spend money. The businesses get paid, and we get nothing. All without our permission.

No wonder we're referred to as users.

This isn't science fiction. It's called social media.

How is this legal? Well, maybe it wasn't, but we realized it too late. We might look back on Web2's data mining and wonder how they got away with it.

People became the product, and in the process, The Matrix felt a little more like science fact. These realities set the stage for Web3—a new type of Internet.

Web3: Open Source

Once the truth on data mining hit mainstream, many people swore they'd never go back. In fact, savvy companies make it a point to separate themselves from the stigma of Web2. Hiro is one such dissenter:

We are no longer limited to the business models that were successful at scale in Web2, such as advertising, subscription, or support-based models.

Instead, Hiro believes there's a competitive advantage to being an open-source company in Web3. They're not alone in this view.

Equinix Metal™ adds to this thinking in an article titled: "Web3 Builders Hope to Fix Open Source, 'Broken' by Web 2.0." The author,

Yevgeniy Sverdlik, puts it plainly. If Web3 succeeds in becoming the third iteration of the internet that its builders envision, one big side effect would be a return of a healthy open source software ecosystem.[17]

Although data mining ranks as one of the uglier byproducts of Web2, there was a silver lining. This global distrust prepared us for open source technology defined by Web3. We experienced quicker adoption and bigger technological breakthroughs as a result.

Bonus Video

COMPONENT

	Web 1 **1991-2004**	**Web 2** **2004-2021**	**Web 3** **2022- ?**
Component	**Advertising**	**Algorithms**	**Artificial Intelligence**

Drive any road in America, and it won't be long before you see billboards lining your path. Roads in other countries tell a similar tale.

This is one component of a physical highway. Since the Internet is a digital highway, we logically witness overlapping metaphors and shared vocabulary words like traffic and gateways.

Each version of the Internet brings with it new components. Specifically in this section, we'll encounter components such as advertising, algorithms, and artificial intelligence.

Web1: Advertising

Back in the beginning of the Internet, one of the primary questions was, who's going to pay for this?

Since Web1 was new, we couldn't grasp the economical component. What better way to learn than trial and error?

According to an article in Teads:

In October 1994 the first online banner ad was born. It simply read: "Have you ever clicked your mouse right HERE? YOU WILL" and was published on HotWired. com—now better known as Wired.com—for a campaign by AT&T. Over four months, 44% of those who saw the ad clicked on it—a percentage most online advertisers could only dream about today.[18]

Banner ads had their time, but they no longer prove effective today. According to an article in The Guardian, "You are more likely to summit Mount Everest than click on a banner ad."[19]

That's pretty bad odds.

Advertisers had a solution when banner ads began to plummet. They created motion, of course. Now rather than respecting our browsing activity, we had to deal with annoying pop-ups.

This is interruption marketing at its finest.

Bestselling author Seth Godin defines this loathsome activity as "communicating messages that interrupt customers while they are doing something of their preference."

Imagine interruption marketing in real life. You're heading to an appointment down a busy city street. You're late and on a mission. Someone jumps in front of you, blocking your path, and asks you to take a quick survey.

How do you feel at that moment? Probably not like completing a survey.

The inventor of the pop-up ad feels your pain. It's why he now apologizes. According to NBC:

> Ethan Zuckerman, creator of the original pop-up ad, which first appeared on Tripod.com in 1997, has a message for the Internet: "I'm sorry." He also thinks that it's time online sites and services moved on from using advertising as the primary means to make money. "I have come to believe that advertising is the original sin of the web," he writes in an article for The Atlantic.[20]

Advertisers didn't leave us in Web2. They only shifted their strategies from pop-ups and banners to stalking and surveillance.

Maybe the original sin just got worse?

Web2: Algorithms

In the same NBC story, Ethan Zuckerman shares how advertising just got more sophisticated in Web2:

> From Facebook tracking us across sites to Google knowing just about everything about you has something to do with advertising. While pervasive ads do enable free services . . . they're reaching the end of their usefulness. People may not like shelling out, but if the alternative is constant surveillance, they might be willing to pay just the same.

Guess what? He's kinda right. But rather than people paying not to be sold to, many people just left the platform altogether.

Web2 experienced a mass exodus from social media platforms. Around the 2020 election, many users got fed up with the polarization. The majority middle was vastly underrepresented. Instead, we were given the choice of two extremes—far right and far left.

Algorithms had something to do with the polarization. According to Sprout Social:

> Social media algorithms are a way of sorting posts in a users' feed based on relevancy instead of publish time. Social networks prioritize which content a user sees in their feed first by the likelihood that they'll actually want to see it. By default, social media algorithms take the reins of determining which content to deliver to you based on your behavior.[21]

Translation?

Although platforms rationalize their motives as pure, the bottom line is that algorithms choose what content to show us. Forget objective truth. We each experience a manipulated version of truth that reinforces our predisposition to certain issues or stories.

This wasn't true with the physical newspapers of the Web1 era. Back then, we all got the same news. Today, our "digital newspaper" is a customized version that hides certain information and highlights other information.

No wonder we feel like much of the world is on different planets. We're not reading the same source. Instead, my truth is mine. And your truth is yours.

There's no meeting in the middle because I can't see what you see, and you can't see what I see. Such polarization created a deeper wedge between us.

Web3: Artificial Intelligence

Artificial Intelligence has been the storyline of science fiction for quite some time. Dictionary.com defines AI plainly:

- the capacity of a computer, robot, or other pro-grammed mechanical device to perform operations and tasks analogous to learning and decision making in humans, as speech recognition or question answering.

- a computer, robot, or other programmed mechanical device having this humanlike capacity

- the branch of computer science involved with the design of computers or other programmed mechanical devices having the capacity to imitate human intelligence and thought.[22]

It's easy to think of AI as something in the distant future. The truth is that AI predates Web3, Web2, and even Web1.

G2, known as the world's largest and most trusted tech marketplace, provides an exhaustive timeline called "A Complete History of Artificial Intelligence."[23] The author reveals:

Between 380 BC and the late 1600s: Various mathematicians, theologians, philosophers, professors, and authors mused about mechanical techniques, calculating machines, and numeral systems that all eventually led to the concept of mechanized "human" thought in non-human beings.

AI has been on our minds for quite a long time, at least the thought of machines performing human functions. Here are a few of those functions, though arguably some far surpass human abilities:[24]

1. Smell

2. Read your mind

3. Recognize objects in images

4. Navigate a map of the London Underground

5. Transcribe speech better than professional transcribers

6. Translate between languages

7. Speak

8. Pick out the bit of a paragraph that answers your question

9. Recognize emotions in images of faces

10. Recognize emotions in speech

11. Drive

12. Fly a drone

13. Predict parking difficulty by area

14. Discover new uses for existing drugs

15. Spot cancer in tissue slides better than human epidemiologists

16. Predict hypoglycemic events in diabetics three hours in advance

17. Identify diabetic retinopathy (a leading cause of blindness) from retinal photos

18. Analyze the genetic code of DNA to detect genomic conditions

19. Detect a range of conditions from images

20. Solve the quantum state of many particles at once

21. Detect crop disease

22. Spray pesticide with pinpoint accuracy

23. Predict crop yields

24. Sort cucumbers

25. Spot burglars in your home

26. Write its own encryption language

27. Predict social unrest 5 days before it happens

28. Unscramble pixelated images

29. Detect malware

30. Verify your identity

31. Anticipate fraudulent payment attacks before they happen

32. Trade stocks

33. Handle insurance claims

34. Predict the outcomes of cases at the European Court of Human Rights with 79% accuracy

35. Do legal case research

36. Do due diligence on M&A deals

37. Flag errors in legal documents

38. Beat 75% of Americans in a visual intelligence test

39. Beat humans at Jeopardy

40. Absolutely nail Super Mario

41. Play Breakout like a total pro

42. Play Go better than humans

43. Beat the best human players at Texas Hold 'Em poker

44. Schedule meetings by email

45. Be your personal trainer

46. Write software unit tests

47. Identify potentially threatening weather

48. Paint a pretty good van Gogh

49. Write poems that get published

50. Write music

51. Design logos

52. Come up with its own recipes

53. Write sports articles for the Associated Press

54. Write film scripts

55. Play soccer badly

56. Recommend songs you'll like

57. Lip-read better than humans

58. Optimize energy usage in air-conditioning units in Google's data centers

59. Become a Twitter troll

60. Collaborate (or become aggressive)

61. Write its own machine learning software[25]

Based on the list above, it almost seems like artificial intelligence is omnipotent. Despite this incredible list, there are some things AI still can't do.[26]

1. Understand cause and effect

2. Reason ethically

3. Learn continuously and adapt on the fly

4. Use "common sense"

And there are a few things AI can't be:[27]

1. Creative

2. Empathetic

3. Dexterous

Without artificial intelligence, Web2 would be in a world of hurt. It helps us locate friends, news, and products. That's a good thing. However, there's a bad side too. AI fuels targeted advertising, accepting or rejecting ads. You can imagine how AI could mess this up.

Case in point.

One of my business clients couldn't discover why his Facebook ad kept getting rejected. Evidently, AI flagged the word execution in his ad, thinking he had violent tendencies. Although the context for the ad was clearly executing strategy, AI thought someone was receiving a deadly threat.

Sometimes AI and Web2 don't mix well together, hence misinformation, echo chambers, and amplified extremist content.[28] For these reasons, I categorized Artificial Intelligence as a component under Web3. Sure, it existed in Web2, but it wasn't perfected.

Many tech experts believe in a forthcoming reimagination of AI when it moves from big tech companies in Web2 to the decentralized creators of Web3.

Forbes Council Member Jeff Wong pulls back the curtain on this possibility. In his article "Cutting Through The Web3 Hype: AI In The Decentralized Web," he writes: "In this decentralized world, users will own their data, privacy will be preserved, censorship will not exist, and rewards will be shared equitably."[29]

Web3 enthusiasts believe we can only move up from Web1 and Web2. Some believe we're already experiencing a sophisticated integration of Web3 and AI, just not across the globe. According to an article on Coindesk, "The science fiction writer William Gibson wrote, 'The future is already here—it's just not evenly distributed' to explain the trajectory of futuristic technology trends. The idea applies perfectly to the intersection of AI and Web 3."[30]

Bonus Video

CONTROL

	Web 1 1991-2004	Web 2 2004-2021	Web 3 2022- ?
Control	**Decentralized**	**Centralized**	**Decentralized**

Who controls the Internet?

Different people give different responses. Common ones include:

- No one

- Everyone

- The Government

- Bill Gates

- Mark Zuckerberg

- Google, Amazon, Facebook, Apple

If you asked people a decade ago, their answers would be different, due to the fact that different versions of the Internet existed. Let's take a brief journey to where things started and where they've shifted.

Web1: Decentralized

In Web1, the Internet felt like the "Wild West." This is because it was. In the nineties, Web1 was running on a fully decentralized infrastructure.[31] An article published on Hackernoon reveals why:

> In Web1 anyone could host a server, and every computer on the internet would act as a relay between browsers and servers. This obviously brought with it pros and cons. Bad actors emerged and—with everything so new and innovative—governing Web1 proved difficult. Web1 was open, decentralized and no one controlled it. If you built something on top of it it was yours and no one could force you to change it.

Decentralization had its place, but it quickly became apparent someone needed to step up control.

Web2: Centralized

Eventually, with so many people onboarding into Web1, governance needed to emerge. Again, we'll borrow the Wild West metaphor. In the beginning, the land is wide open and much like a free for all. But, when the people converge, rules and regulations are enforced for everyone's safety.

As people started building applications on the internet, a set of standards emerged to enable interoperability: websites were all built using HTML so that anyone would need a browser to view the data, emails were all in the same format and accessible via pop3 and IMAP protocols so that anyone could build an email client that could send and receive emails from other clients, chat rooms used IRC, calendars used CalDav, and so forth. Effectively, anyone could build software that interacted with other existing software simply by virtue of following the same standard.[32]

We know what happened.

Businesses formed. Power grew. And eventually, Big Tech ended up with control. The Internet shifted from decentralization to centralization.

Centralization brings advantages like support and simplicity. But in a centralized Internet, politics arose, and censorship prevailed. We witnessed abuse so significant that documentaries began popping up. The advantages of centralization faded, and the need for decentralization became the rallying cry of everyday users.

Web3: Decentralized

In a decentralized Internet, power is given back to the people. Privacy is regained, and the "middle man" is removed from the equation. Web3 Internet has been called frictionless and trustless.

Angel investor Rand Hindi believes, "We are now at a critical juncture for the internet, where a new technology is radically changing the game: blockchain."[33]

Many share in this sentiment. Insiders feel like we're on the edge of something big. Chris Dixon of Andreessen

Horowitz (a16z), one of the top venture capital firms in Web3, certainly does. "I think Web3 is not only better for the world, but it's also going to beat Web2. It's going to be more popular because the people get really excited when they actually get to participate."[34]

Decentralization is more than a trendy term. It provides real benefits, according to Doug Petkanics. Six in fact:

Users don't have to put trust in a central authority.

There is less likely to be a single point of failure.

There is less censorship.

Decentralized networks are more likely to be open development platforms.

There is potential for network ownership alignment.

Decentralized networks can be more meritocratic.[35]

Bonus Video

CURRENCY

	Web 1 1991-2004	Web 2 2004-2021	Web 3 2022- ?
Currency	Credit Cards	Payment Aggregators	Cryptocurrencies

Today, most people are familiar with online shopping. Most of us experience it on a daily basis for personal and professional purposes. We pay our taxes and our charitable donations via the Internet. Our water, electricity, and sanitation can be paid via online payments.

Even our groceries, prescriptions, and cleaning supplies leverage subscription-based payments.

Imagine a world before Internet currencies. Most people don't want to try. We've gotten too comfortable enjoying the convenience, security, and simplicity of online commerce.

Web 1: Credit Cards

I remember some older family members refusing to use credit cards to make online purchases. Some are still afraid and vow they'll never jump on board. Their commonsense approach is understandable.

These people grew up in a world where money was something you held in your pocket or purse. The thought of entering a private credit card number into a screen on a computer seems frightening, especially in a world with constant headlines of hackers, scammers, and bad actors.

Not everyone stayed scared. Eventually, someone stepped up. Phil Brandenberger was the first to make the leap on August 11, 1994. This day will go in history, at least Internet history.

According to VISA, this was the day the first ecommerce payment was made on its network.[36]

In the The New York Times article titled "Attention Shoppers: Internet is Open," readers learned about the details surrounding the first purchase on the Internet:

At noon yesterday, Phil Brandenberger of Philadelphia went shopping for a compact audio disk, paid for it with his credit card and made history.

Moments later, the champagne corks were popping in a small two-story frame house in Nashua, N.H. There, a team of young cyberspace entrepreneurs celebrated what was apparently the first retail transaction on the Internet using a readily available version of powerful data encryption software designed to guarantee privacy.

From his work station in Philadelphia, Mr. Brandenburger logged onto the computer in Nashua, and used a secret code to send his Visa credit card number to pay $12.48, plus shipping costs, for the compact disk "Ten Summoners' Tales" by the rock musician Sting.[37]

Before the Internet, shopping was quite a different experience. For starters, you needed to leave your home. "Shoppers did not have the luxury of buying anything they wanted from the comfort of their sofas, and long lines and fragmented payment technology made for frustrating checkout experiences."[38]

Who wants to stand in long lines?

Who wants to visit a store only to find out the store is sold out of inventory?

It didn't take long to see the practicality of online shopping. The major hurdle was security. "Experts have long seen such iron-clad security as a necessary first step before commercial transactions can become common on the Internet, the global computer network."[39]

In 1994, all of this changed. Credit cards became the new currency of the Internet, albeit a slow adoption. That same year many other businesses awakened to the new possibilities.

In 1994:[40]

- Amazon.com sold the first book online, evidently not a real page-turner (Fluid Concepts and Creative Analogies).

- Pizza Hut started online sales through a pilot project called PizzaNet out of Santa Cruz, California.

- Neiman Marcus introduced the first payments-oriented gift card in 1994 (Blockbuster and Kmart Cash were a close second.).

Web1 showed us the possibilities with Internet currencies.

Web2: Payment Aggregators

As you know from the Web Comparison Chart™ back at the beginning of this book, Web2 spans from 2004–2021. Much happened in those years, including the adoption of payment aggregators.

Payment aggregators are "a service that sees all payments flow through a single, centralized merchant account, without the involvement of traditional banks or financial institutions. It condenses the management of all electronic payments into a single online portal."[41]

Confinity—later named PayPal—first offered a type of payment aggregator option back in 1998. It was the first to do so. Payment aggregators started slowly in Web1. However, in Web2, they became a top choice for exchanging currency.

The numbers reveal how ecommerce has overtaken offline commerce:

- E-retail totaled over $5.2 trillion in 2021.[42]

- Cross-border ecommerce sales worldwide grew over 20% in 2020.[43]

- US ecommerce grew by over 14% in 2021.[44]

- Amazon's net profit increased by over 80% in 2020.[45]

- Over half of consumers use smartphones for shopping.[46]

- There are over 3.8 billion ecommerce users worldwide.[47]

- By the year 2040, it is estimated that 95% of all global purchases will be done through ecommerce.[48]

Payment aggregators are popular for several reasons. Square, one of the most popular payment aggregators, provides four reasons why.[49]

1. **Easy, instant setup:** The traditional merchant application process is complex and time-consuming, filled with credit checks, PCI compliance checks, personal guarantees, business model analysis, and more. Setup with a payment aggregator, meanwhile, can be completed in mere minutes.

2. **Transparent and affordable:** Payment aggregators like Square offer a simple, transparent and affordable fee structure. You know exactly how much you'll pay for the service—usually a small percentage of each transaction, rather than a flat fee—allowing you to budget better.

3. **Take payment the way you want:** Merchant aggregators allow you to take payment however you want. Square, for example, offers the hardware and software to take payments in-person, online, over the phone, and via card, contactless or transfer.

4. **Safe and secure:** A payment aggregator's main focus is to ensure the safety and security of its service. You can trust Square to handle your business's money and to do so in a fully compliant way.

This payment aggregator technology helped me as a new entrepreneur more than a decade ago. As an author, I sold books at my speaking events and customers wanted to pay me with their credit cards.

I visited my local bank in hope of a solution. They tried signing me up with a long contract so I could "rent" their bulky equipment and swipe credit cards. Even back then, it felt clunky. So instead, I looked into other solutions.

I chose Square because of their simple card reader option. I popped the device into the headphone jack on my phone and ran all transactions through the payment aggregator platform.

Despite the benefits, payment aggregators had some cons too:

1. **Account Holds:** A payment gateway that allows for instant processing means a higher risk for chargebacks. Aggregators can be slightly paranoid about account holds. Even the smallest hint of irregular activity can lock your account. This extreme caution could keep a business from making a sale if the timing is wrong.

2. **Delayed Funds:** It's ultimately up to the aggregator how long they keep your funds. They have their own monthly fees to pay, so if they need to float your money, they will. Most merchants are paid within one to three business days from the transaction, but it's not something set in stone. They can choose to release funds in a timely manner, or some can hold your money up to thirty days. This is not a common practice, however, because most don't want to lose customers.

3. **Lower Limits:** Aggregators are usually charged based on gross processing volume. That means they pass on limits to merchants. If you use this method, your processing limits will be lower than going with a separate merchant account.[50]

These cons, and several other reasons, paved the way for cryptocurrencies and Web3.

Web3: Cryptocurrencies

I didn't understand cryptocurrencies at first because I didn't understand money. Maybe this is true for you too.

In my country, the USA, we use fiat money, also called the US Dollar. Fiat money is not a term we use often. Check out these definitions which describe fiat:

- **Dictionary:** Inconvertible paper money made legal tender by a government decree.[51]

- **Investopedia:** Government-issued currency that is not backed by a physical commodity, such as gold or silver, but rather by the government that issued it.[52]

Maybe like me, you grew up with people lying to you about the US Dollar. They told me it was backed by gold. Lied is a strong word, and it implies motives. Therefore, it's probably better to say these people misinformed me.

The US dollar was backed by gold until August 15, 1971. On that date, President Nixon decided to take the dollar off the gold standard. Since I was born after this date, I've never known a dollar backed by gold.

If it's not backed by the dollar, then what's it backed by? If you want the truth, then it's backed by nothing. Of course, few people admit that so they provide the official, complex answer:

In contrast to commodity-based money like gold coins or paper bills redeemable for precious metals, fiat money is backed entirely by the full faith and trust in the government that issued it. One reason this has merit is that governments demand that you pay taxes in the fiat money it issues. Since everybody needs to pay taxes, or else face stiff penalties or prison, people will accept it in exchange. Other theories of money, such as the credit theory, suggest that since all money is a credit-debt relation, it does not matter if money is backed by anything to maintain value.[53]

No matter how we spin it, once we realize fiat money is backed by nothing, then other forms of currency can offer a compelling alternative. Remember, the value of fiat money is derived from the relationship between supply and demand.[54] But so is cryptocurrency.

In the case of Bitcoin, there will only be 21 million ever. Since the US government can print as much money as it wants without creating new value, fiat money will always decrease in value. On the flip side, because the amount of Bitcoin is scarce and can never increase, its value will always increase.

Many people believe cryptocurrency is superior because it requires value creation to create more of it. This value is often expressed by "miners" creating new cryptocurrency tokens. "This process involves using software to verify the block on the blockchain to decentralize and form the token. To verify the blockchain, participants need to use computing power and solve transaction-related algorithms. However, there is a competition to mine certain cryptocurrencies largely due to the miners racing each other to verify the next block, which can make it more difficult to mine."[55]

Bitcoin is one form of cryptocurrency, but there are thousands of types of cryptocurrencies, including Ethereum and Binance Coin. Cryptocurrencies are just one of many examples of decentralized finance (DeFi), an emerging financial technology based on secure distributed ledgers.

If you're unfamiliar with an official definition of cryptocurrency, here's a simple one:

It's an encrypted data string that denotes a unit of currency. It is monitored and organized by a peer-to- peer network called a blockchain, which also serves as a secure ledger of transactions, e.g., buying, selling, and transferring. Unlike physical money, cryptocurrencies are decentralized, which means they are not issued by governments or other financial institutions.

Cryptocurrencies are created (and secured) through cryptographic algorithms that are maintained and confirmed in a process called mining, where a network of computers or specialized hardware such as application- specific integrated circuits (ASICs) process and validate the transactions. The process incentivizes the miners who run the network with the cryptocurrency.[56]

For non-technological people, these last two paragraphs can simply come across as jargon. This isn't helpful. Of course, you can take a deep dive into cryptocurrency to understand the finer points. Certainly, volumes have been written on this topic. However, for the purpose of this book, my desire is to show why cryptocurrency is rising in popularity and utility.

We can debate which is superior and why—cryptocurrency or fiat currency. Although this may be a worthy debate, before we utter a word, we must understand that all currencies are based upon faith.

Money has taken many forms through the ages: shells, wheels, beads, and even cows.[57] These currencies were based upon adoption and acceptance too. However, overnight currencies can tank. Look no further than the devaluing of Confederate Dollars ("graybacks") immediately after the Civil War.[58]

Once we are honest about the way money is valued, then we can objectively explore which is better, fiat money or cryptocurrency. Although this is a matter only you can decide for yourself, exploring the pros and cons of cryptocurrency will help you in your decision process.[59]

Pros of Bitcoin	Cons of Bitcoin
Accessibility and Liquidity	Volatility
User Anonymity and Transparency	No Government Regulation
Independence from Central Authority	Irreversible
High Return Potential	Limited Use

The majority of popular Web1 currencies (credit cards) and Web2 currencies (payment aggregators) are based upon fiat money. Rising inflation and the ability of governments to print endless money threaten this system. Eventually, like all societies before us, our greed and carelessness will tank this currency.

For these reasons, despite its volatility, cryptocurrency is quickly becoming the currency of choice in Web3.

Bonus Video

DANGER

	Web 1 1991-2004	Web 2 2004-2021	Web 3 2022- ?
Danger	Phishing	Hacking	Deepfaking

Technology and progress always come with danger but so does staying status quo and failing to change. Each version of the Internet comes with unique dangers, some worse than others.

Web 1: Phishing

Phishing began in 1995 with all targets pointed at America Online (AOL), the number-one provider of Internet access. Millions of people logged on to the service each day. Bad actors stole users' passwords and used algorithms to create randomized credit card numbers.[60] Their spree was short-lived when AOL created security measures to prevent the ability to use randomly generated credit card numbers.

The term "phishing" first appeared on January 2, 1996, in a Usenet newsgroup called AOHell. Seventeen-year-old Koceilah Rekouche, known online as "Da Chronic," created a toolkit that provided a new DLL for the AOL client, a credit card number generator, email bomber, IM bomber, Punter, and a basic set of instructions.[61]

His ill intentions equipped people to misuse the Internet for personal gain. The term phishing caught on, replacing the "ph" in place of the "f." Some of the earliest hackers were known as phreaks. Phreaking refers to the exploration, experimenting, and study of telecommunication systems.

Phishing reached global status with a phishing scheme called the Love Bug on May 4, 2000. Although it ended up infecting about 45 million Windows PCs, it started on one machine in the Philippines.

The message preyed on curiosity with a simple subject line: "ILOVEYOU." The body of the email said, "Kindly check the attached LOVELETTER coming from me."

> Those who could not resist unearthing their secret crush, opened what they thought was a harmless .txt file, only to unleash a worm that did damage on the local machine. The worm overwrote image files and sent a copy of itself to all the user's contacts in their Outlook address book. 'LoveBug' showed how to get spam to send itself and that, with a cleverly designed virus that preyed on human psychology and technical failings, malware could rack up enormous numbers of victims.[62]

Today, 3.1 billion spoofed emails are sent every day.[63] With built-in spam filters standard through most email providers, bad actors needed more sophisticated strategies, hence the shift to hacking in Web2.

Web2: Hacking

In the Web2 era, Internet users became more wary. We adopted standard computer hygiene practices:

Don't open email attachments.
Don't click on links.

Such caution only emboldened bad actors. As a result, they took more aggressive measures with good old-fashioned hacking.

There's a difference between phishing and hacking. Both share similar goals, acquiring personal information for financial gain. However, both are different in the means of achieving that goal.

With a phish, the victim is baited into voluntarily giving out their information. The crime comes from the malicious intent and falsification of credibility. When it comes to phishing, there is a clear sense of false advertising or fraudulent identification in order to lure victims into giving up their personal information.[64]

With hacking, victims don't intentionally disclose their private information. Hacking often occurs without a victim's knowledge. "The perpetrator will take over your computer system in order to access private information."[65]

Although I've never succumbed to a phishing attack, I've come close. Recently, I made a purchase at a local sporting goods store. The salesperson was so kind I went out of my way to complete a survey where I shared about his stellar service. This was out of the ordinary, but so was the way he fixed my botched delivery date.

A few days later, I received an email from the same sporting goods store. The email looked legitimate because it made its way past my spam blocker. The email invited me to complete a simple survey in exchange for a quality backpack. It used the normal psychological tactics:

- Thanks for your customer loyalty.

- You've been chosen to take a simple survey.

- Choose your gift at the end of the survey, including this incredible backpack.

The more I read, the more fishy—or phishy—it smelled. As a result, I quickly deleted the email. No harm done.

I wish I could say the same about hacking. This past year, a hacker took over one of our social media pages. Since I have an international team with several members, identifying the security breach wasn't easy.

I hired a competent cybersecurity team who helped us "beef up" our security standards. Although they did a fantastic job, we only got our page back because a friend of a friend worked at that social media company.

Bottom line, hacking is alive and well in any version of the Internet. Cybercrime comes with a hefty price tag, that rises 15% every year.

According to multiple sources, cybercrime costs the world trillions of dollars.[66]

Web3: Deepfaking

Phishing and hacking do plenty of damage, but there's a danger even more fatal—deepfaking.

I noticed it around 2018. Maybe you did too?

Distrust mounted. We began questioning if what we were seeing or reading was true. Fake news skyrocketed.

Honesty in journalism has always been difficult. However, the amount of media channels and the amount of journalists have historically kept the problem in check. Centralization does shine in this regard.

However, Web3 is a decentralized Internet. Combine that with our advances in mobile computing, wearable technology, and 5G capability, and suddenly anyone can say anything at any time, anywhere. Without accountability, who knows what to believe? Cynicism and skepticism soar and deepfaking abounds.

Do you know a deepfake when you see it?

Have you seen Barack Obama call Donald Trump a "complete dip#$%@," or Mark Zuckerberg brag about having "total control of billions of people's stolen data," or witnessed Jon Snow's moving apology for the dismal ending to Game of Thrones?[67]

Answer yes, and you've seen a deepfake. The 21st century's answer to Photoshopping, deepfakes use a form of artificial intelligence called deep learning to make images of fake events, hence the name deepfake. The problem with deepfaking is that it looks and sounds authentic.

Without truth, a society cannot survive.

Current deepfaking often attacks women. The AI firm Deeptrace found 15,000 deepfake videos online in September 2019, a near doubling over nine months. A staggering 96% were pornographic, and 99% of those mapped faces from female celebrities onto porn stars. As Danielle Citron, a professor of law at Boston University, puts it: "Deepfake technology is being weaponized against women."[68]

Deepfakes erode trust. People no longer know what to believe. Terrorists understand this, and some leverage this technology as part of their espionage arsenal:

> A non-existent Bloomberg journalist, "Maisy Kinsley," who had a profile on LinkedIn and Twitter, was probably a deepfake. Another LinkedIn fake, "Katie Jones," claimed to work at the Center for Strategic and International Studies, but is thought to be a deepfake created for a foreign spying operation.[69]

Despite the dangers of Web3, we must find our way forward. Opting for an offline existence is nearly impossible.

Bonus Video

ECONOMY

	Web 1 1991-2004	Web 2 2004-2021	Web 3 2022- ?
Economy	Information	Attention	Creator

In business, we're told to follow the money. This is smart advice when evaluating the Internet too. Each version focuses on a different type of economy.

Web 1: Information

In Web1, users sought information. With products and services in mind, they hunted for data. Whether ordering food or researching for their next mode of transportation, they wanted to know the toppings for their pizza or their paint color for their new truck.

Web2: Attention

In one of my other books Unhackable, I explored the attention economy. When I began researching for the book back in 2014, I was deeply alarmed at how technology distracted us and kept us from achieving our dreams.

It got worse.

I discovered this was intentional. Companies profited off of our attention, designing apps and devices with this in mind. I'll include an excerpt from Unhackable that exposes the conspiracy:[70]

Welcome to the Attention Economy—where you are the product. In this digital landscape, they keep score with eyeballs and eardrums. Focus is everything, and they're willing to fight for yours. They no longer track the cash. That's too far down the line. They know what precedes the purchasing decision.

Your attention.

We call it paying attention for a reason. Businesses, politicians, and even non-profits know your thoughts are worth a price, and they'll do almost anything to gain market share. Social media keeps score with likes, views, shares, subscribers, and comments.

The metrics may differ, but the strategy doesn't. If they can divert or distract you, they win. If they can sideline or sabotage your plans, they succeed. It's connected to the Altered States Economy (how we use various sources to shift our state of mind), and according to research done by Steven Kotler and Jamie Wheal in Stealing Fire, it represents four trillion dollars. Ironically, we're choosing to get hacked, and we're footing the bill for it.

But getting hacked comes with a price more costly than dollars and cents. By adopting roles as consumers rather than creators, we fail to embody our divine destiny.

Web3: Creator

If Web3 is starting to feel like a revolution, this is because many insiders believe it is. Web2 taught us the dangers of unchecked power and centralization. We all felt the limitations, and we could no longer turn a blind eye.

Web3 is a return to many of the best parts of Web1 but with more maturity, experience, and upgrades.

According to *Cointelegraph*:

> The upcoming Web3 paradigm of the creator economy aims to enable creators to build their own independent "open economy" where they can co-own it with their fans and directly monetize it without looking to any third party. As some field experts assume, if this model succeeds, we will enter a new era of wealth generation where creators will no longer be just the products. Instead, they will become new economies.[71]

This creator economy thrives because of certain characteristics intrinsic to Web3. This new version of the Internet centers on an ecosystem of technology products that are:[72]

1. **Decentralized:** Blockchain-powered networks store data across distributed devices. No central authority that governs decision-making. No single centralized server that controls the data.

2. Trustless: The blockchain serves as an immutable record. No need to place your trust in a stranger. No need to use a third-party intermediary for transactions.

3. **Permissionless:** Open networks let everyone participate in the consensus process. No gatekeeper has

control or the power to bar anyone from accessing the Internet.

4. **Interoperable:** The ability of different systems, devices, applications, or products to connect and communicate in a coordinated way, without effort from the end user.[73]

5. Insiders are witnessing this compound effect in real time. It feels as though we are on the precipice of a "Technological Renaissance."

Bonus Video

EXPERIENCE

	Web 1 1991-2004	Web 2 2004-2021	Web 3 2022- ?
Experience	Static	Dynamic	Interactive

The Internet is an experience. However, each version of the Internet provides a different one.

Web 1: Static

Static: *characterized by a lack of movement, animation, or progression.*[74]

We came to the first version of the Internet with the desire for information. As a result, most websites provided static information: hours of operation, menus, or lists of products and services. If you visited a website and read information, chances are you could come back to the same website months later and read the same information.

Web2: Dynamic

Dynamic: *marked by usually continuous and productive activity or change.*[75]

We came to the second version of the Internet with the desire for interaction. As a result, we could connect with people and contribute content. If you visited a platform and interacted, chances are you could come back to the same platform days later and your experience would be completely different.

Web3: Interactive

Interactive: *involving the actions or input of a user.*[76]

We came to the third version of the Internet with the desire for participation. As a result, we could integrate and embody the Internet. If you visited a metaverse and created within it, chances are you could come back to the same metaverse seconds later and change reality for you and those around you.

Bonus Video

EXTREME

	Web 1 1991-2004	Web 2 2004-2021	Web 3 2022- ?
Extreme	Dot-Com Bubble	The Social Dilemma	Transhumanism

Turns out, too much of a good thing can be a bad thing. Any version of the Internet brings the potential of certain extremes.

Web 1: Dot-Com Bubble

As a teenager in the 1990s, I didn't pay much attention to the Internet or the stock market. Years later, I heard notorious stories about the dot-com era. Evidently, these types of companies had three things in common:[77]

1. They vowed to "change the world."

2. They experienced incredibly-high valuations.

3. They became wildly unprofitable.

The dot-com bubble of the late 1990s and early 2000s included unchecked projections and bullish investments. Excitement about the future of tech attracted a massive amount of attention from venture capitalists and traditional investors. Debt financing was easier to acquire, further fueling the Internet's speculative growth

Back then, most people saw Web1 as a source of endless possibilities. Internet-enabled businesses promised to change our homes, relationships, and jobs.

Eventually, these streams of easy money dried up, and the industry imploded, causing many tech companies to go under. Between 2001 and early 2004, Silicon Valley alone lost 200,000 jobs. A whole segment of workers who bet their careers on tech was left unemployed. This ushered in a several-year bear market affecting the entire stock market—not only the technology sector.

Looking back, the dot-com extreme took place for several reasons:

1. **Adoption:** "The dot-com era was doomed to failure simply because there were too many companies chasing what at the time were too few users. When the bubble burst in 2000, there were only around 400 million people online worldwide. Ten years later, there would be more than 2 billion (best estimates peg the current number of internet users at 3.4 billion)."[78]

2. **Advertising:** Venture Capitalists poured money into companies that advertised. These companies then spent more on advertising. More people saw these

websites, which led to more money being invested and thus more money spent on advertising. This created a vicious cycle. Some start-ups were spending up to 90% of their investment in this way.[79]

3. **Abundance:** Eventually, an Initial Public Offering (IPO) would happen, with the public buying shares in these highly valued companies. Cheap funds obtainable through very low interest rates made capital easily accessible.[80]

In the end, all this Web1 hopium proved to be mostly hype. Of course, someone needed to fund the frenzy. Overly optimistic investors couldn't escape paying the bill.

Some good came out of the whole debacle, though. We learned a more mature approach to life online, and we took this knowledge into Web2.

Web2: The Social Dilemma

When many of the creators of social media won't let their kids use the exact same technology they created—perhaps we should be concerned?

This was one of the major premises of the 2020 American docudrama film directed by Jeff Orlowski. The film revealed the extremes of Web2 and specifically how social media:

- Promotes addictive tendencies based on its design
- Profits from our attention
- Manipulates people's views, emotions, and behavior
- Spreads conspiracy theories and disinformation
- Affects mental health in particular adolescents and rising teen suicide rates

The documentary served as a wake-up call to many, demonstrating how social media platforms alter newsfeeds and, in some cases, truth to keep users addicted, emotionally charged, and polarized. These tactics leveraged the attention economy to keep advertisers spending and users buying products and services.

Unfortunately, all versions of the Internet, including Web2, come with the potential for harmful extremes.

Web3: Transhumanism

Ever hear this plot? Humans and machines merge into an integrated species, giving the new creature otherworldly abilities. Philosophical questions emerge.

- Where does humanity end?
- Where does artificial intelligence begin?
- Does the new being have a conscience, a soul, or the potential for empathy?

This transhumanistic story arc dominates many sci-fi movies. The plot changes regarding how humans and machines merge:

- A surgery?
- A love affair?
- An experiment?
- An attempt for world power?

But regardless of how it begins, transhumanism usually ends the same predictable way—a dystopian nightmare.

Does it have to end this way? For all our sakes, we'd better hope not. Here's why. Transhuman is no longer fiction but fact—and one day this extreme could be as culturally accepted as a haircut.

According to Britannica:

Transhumanism is a social and philosophical movement devoted to promoting the research and development of robust human-enhancement technologies. Such technologies would augment or increase human sensory reception, emotive ability, or cognitive capacity as well as radically improve human health and extend human life spans. Such modifications resulting from the addition of biological or physical technologies would be more or less permanent and integrated into the human body.[81]

If you're unfamiliar with the concept of transhumanism, you're not alone. But you'd better get ready because expressions of transhumanism are popping up all around.

For starters, there's Neil Harbisson, the world's first true cyborg, the man with an antenna sticking out of his head. He fits the definition "that [scientist] Manfred Clynes gave for 'cyborg' in 1960."[82] In order to explore and survive in new environments, we have to change ourselves instead of changing our environment.

Harbisson's struggle with achromatopsia, which causes him to see the world in solely black and white, motivated him to devise a solution by implanting an antenna in his head.[83] He has been able to "hear" visible and invisible wavelengths of light. An antenna-like sensor implanted in his head translates different wavelengths into vibrations on his skull, which he then perceives as sound.[84]

Some might view his antenna as a technological enhancement, similar to a hearing aid or contact lenses, but Harbisson doesn't call it wearable technology. He refers to it as a new organ. "I don't feel like I use or carry technology, as I am technology."[85] It seems the UK government also agrees with him, allowing him to include the antenna in his passport, making him the world's first recognized cyborg."[86]

Harbisson is a transhumanist, part of a growing movement that believes the next stage in human evolution is merging with technology. Such proponents believe humans need to design and modify their own bodies. Harbisson has become a magnet for teens who experience an intense desire to become cyborgs when they turn eighteen years old. "They have felt their whole lives that they're more than just a human. Just like transgenders have the feeling that the gender they were born with wasn't the one that suits them best."[87]

In previous generations, it might be easy to write off these desires to become a machine as fringe. "But thanks to recent scientific developments in areas such as biotechnology, information technology, and nanotechnology, humanity may be on the cusp of an enhancement revolution."[88]

According to the Pew Research Center:

Some talk about what might be called "humanity plus"–people who are still recognizably human, but much smarter, stronger, and healthier. Others speak of "post-humanity," and predict that dramatic advances in genetic engineering and machine technology may ultimately allow people to become conscious machines–not recognizably human, at least on the outside.

In my day, getting a tattoo or a nose piercing was considered fringe behavior. Today, we're enhancing our bodies with technology.

Society seems to be open to transhumanism. At the Brave New World international conference, often attended by artists, scientists, and philosophers, nearly 75% of the audience voted that they would be open "to 'improve' their body or mind using technology."[89]

Transhumanist-friendly companies are popping up all over. CyborgNest develops "innovative human augmentation technologies to enhance people's abilities."[90]

As technology progresses, we unlock more and more superhuman powers. A few of the popular human-machine integrations include abilities to:[91]

- Sense direction based upon the magnetic pull (available as an implant or a wearable called NorthSense)

- Feel earthquakes anywhere on the planet

- Detect a change in the atmosphere through air pressure

- Touch—using the bebionic hand—a prosthetic

- See—leveraging the eyeborg project—a prosthetic

- Run—using the mind-controlled bionic leg—a prosthetic

Most people applaud a brain-computer interface prosthetic leg for people born without a leg or who lose one due to an accident. However, when those superhuman legs allow you to squat thousands of pounds, run one-minute miles, and scale mountains, we might have to confront a very real possibility.

In order to attain post-human powers, some people will request amputations and significant surgeries. Forget breast augmentation and BOTOX®. Some humans may want to transplant their brains into new machine-enhanced bodies.

The Alcor Life Extension Foundation in Scottsdale, Arizona is preparing the way. Founded in 1972, this non-profit organization sees its mission as bringing cryonics to the world. Upon physical death, Alcor clients' brains are frozen in "long-term cryogenic dewars," where they await new technology which will one day initiate their "resurrection." According to Alcor, their clients don't die. Rather, they're simply "suspended."

Alcor's website presents four components that serve as its guiding principles:[92]

1. Preserving Life

   Cryonics is the practice of preserving life by pausing the dying process using subfreezing temperatures with the intent of restoring good health with medical technology in the future.

2. Pausing the Dying Process

   The definitions of death change over time as medical understanding and technology improve. Someone who would've been declared dead decades ago may still have a chance today. Death used to be when a person's heart stopped, then when their heart couldn't be restarted, and is now being extended further.

3. Modern Science

   Cryonics sounds like science fiction, but it's based on modern science. Life can be stopped and restarted if its basic structures can be preserved. Vitrification can preserve biological structure very well—much better than freezing. Methods for repairing biological structure at the molecular level can now be foreseen.

4. Cryonics within Reach

We're making cryonics accessible to everyone. With low monthly dues and an insurance policy, you're all set. When the time comes, we'll perform your cryopreservation at our state-of-the-art facilities. Patients are kept in secure, long-term cryogenic dewars until revival. Welcome to your future.

Naturally, the extremes of Web3 like transhumanism raise all kinds of questions. "Many thinkers from different disciplines and faith traditions worry that radical changes will lead to people who are no longer either physically or psychologically human."[93] For this reason, "there is significant philosophical, ethical, and religious opposition to transhumanism."[94] However, that opposition is turning into greater acceptance with every day that passes.

Bonus Video

FUNCTION

	Web 1 1991-2004	Web 2 2004-2021	Web 3 2022- ?
Function	Reading	Writing	Executing

The creator of the World Wide Web should be the one to identify the function of all three versions of the Internet. But does such a person exist?

According to the Internet Hall of Fame®, he does, and his name is Tim Berners-Lee.[95]

Web 1: Reading

According to Berners-Lee, Web1 is the "read-only web."

The first version of the Internet invites us to consume. We searched for information, and then we read it. "There was very little in the way of user interaction or content generation."[96]

Web2: Writing

According to Berners-Lee, Web2 is the "read-write web."

The second version of the Internet invited us to contribute. Besides reading, we created content and interacted with other people.

"As examples, look at YouTube and MySpace, which rely on user submissions."[97] (If you don't know what MySpace was, you can google it or ask someone older than you. It was/is a thing.)

Web3: Executing

According to Berners-Lee, Web3 is the "read-write-execute web."

The third version of the Internet invited us to create. "It is a version of the web that gives users the power to create and execute tools and software, rather than depending on other people for software."[98]

Bonus Video

GOVERNANCE

	Web 1 1991-2004	Web 2 2004-2021	Web 3 2022- ?
Governance	Individuals	Big Tech	DAOs

Who governs the Internet?

If you google search this question, you'll quickly find an answer:

> No one person, company, organization or government runs the Internet. It is a globally distributed network comprising many voluntarily interconnected autonomous networks. It operates without a central governing body with each constituent network setting and enforcing its own policies.[99]

This is the very definition of decentralization, a topic we explored earlier in the book. On October 1, 2016, a historic event took place, which further illustrated the point, in case there were any doubters. According to Business Insider:

> The U.S. government finally handed over control of the world wide web's "phonebook" to the Internet Corporation for Assigned Names and Numbers (ICANN) after almost 20 years of transition. The ICANN, a nonprofit organization composed of stakeholders from government organizations, members of private companies, and internet users from all over the world, now has direct control over the Internet Assigned Numbers Authority (IANA), the body that manages the web's domain name system (DNS).[100]

Web 1: Individuals

In the beginning, it was every person for himself or herself. Individuals practiced self-governance—or lack thereof. Some did well, and some did poorly. As with any emerging tech, governments, policies, and standards were slow to catch up.

Web2: Big Tech

Around 2013, at the height of Web2, the term "Big Tech" surfaced and not in a good way.[101] This was the same year that Edward Snowden leaked information about NSA surveillance. Distrust soared and articles popped, like this one titled: "Big Tobacco, Big Pharma. Big Tech? The rise of a new epithet, and what it means for Silicon Valley."

Big Tech captured the title as the monopoly of our generation due to these compelling issues:

1. Privacy
2. Market power

3. Free speech

4. Censorship

5. National security and law enforcement

Watchdog organizations included Big Tech as part of their advocacy agenda. One such organization, Freedom House, posted a warning cry: "In the high-stakes battle between states and technology companies, the rights of internet users have become the main casualties."[102]

Internet users felt the loss of their rights. Governments literally intervened, with antitrust investigations launched by the Department of Justice and Federal Trade Commission in the United States and the European Commission.

Web3: DAOs

New versions of the Internet enable new forms of governance. The most popular choice in Web3 seems to be decentralized autonomous organizations (DAOs). Power is distributed across token holders who collectively cast votes for the management and decision-making of an entity.

The Constitution DAO is one such example. It emerged in 2021 with the single goal—purchasing a copy of the US Constitution. (Refer back to the introduction for more on this noteworthy event.)

DAOs function as a vehicle to carry out decentralized governance. These organizations rely heavily on smart contracts and blockchain technology for voting and activity. Cryptocurrencies and digital assets such as NFTs often play a role in this multi-layer Web3 governance experience.

According to Forbes:

Uniswap is one of the biggest and most popular DAOs and operates as a cryptocurrency exchange built on the Ethereum blockchain. Anyone can become a member by holding the UNI token, which gives voting rights on the way the organization is run and administered.[103]

Universities, churches, sports teams, and communities could one day adopt a DAO-type structure to govern themselves. Since each of these examples integrate a digital and physical experience, DAOs may prove to be a preferred mode of governance.

Bonus Video

IMAGE

	Web 1 1991-2004	Web 2 2004-2021	Web 3 2022-?
Image	Clip Art	Videos	Gaming Engines

The majority of people are visual learners—sixty-five percent of the planet. The rest are auditory and kinesthetic (movement) learners.

Everyone uses all three modalities, but one is dominant. This concept is called the VAK learning style (visual, auditory, kinesthetic) and it indicates how we receive new information and experiences.[104]

Since humans are so visual, when the Internet integrated images, learning rapidly accelerated. The saying "a picture is worth 1,000 words" became our reality propelling us into new levels of thought.

Web 1: Clip Art

You have to start somewhere and when it comes to images, Web1 started with clip art. Most experts identify mechanical paste-up as its inefficient predecessor. But, "Most publishers would move away from mechanical paste-up by the early 1990s. Desktop publishing software such as Adobe Indesign or QuarkXPress made print design much less tedious."[105]

Clip art wasn't pretty, but visual integration helped users learn faster and easier. Although primitive, clip art also paved the way for advertisement, a much-needed economic model essential to massive Internet adoption.

Web2: Videos

Video took the Internet to another level.

According to experts, "The Dancing Baby" was the video that took the world by storm. Back in 1996, "The 3D-rendered, diaper-clad baby doing some version of the Cha Cha is widely known as the first viral video or meme."[106]

Looking back, that particular video isn't a masterpiece, but for some reason, it captivated the attention of millions of people and spread like wildfire, even appearing on the hit TV show Ally McBeal.

Although this video launched in Web1, it took many years for videos to reign supreme as a preferred medium for Internet content. Several major events propelled the adoption of online videos. On September 10, 2003, Adobe released the first version of Flash Video. This container file format delivered digital video content over the Internet.

Apple co-founder Steve Jobs hated Flash Video, saying it was "unreliable, outdated, and proprietary, and criticized the program for sapping battery power, failing to support touch-based devices and having technical and security drawbacks."[107]

For this reason, many people point to YouTube as the platform that ushered in video as the mainstream medium. YouTube was registered on February 14, 2005, by Steve Chen, Chad Hurley, and Jawed Karim, three former employees of the American ecommerce company PayPal.[108]

It's difficult to argue with the firepower of video on the Internet:

- 97.8% of US internet users aged between 18 and 24 consider themselves to be digital video viewers.[109]

- 54% of consumers want to see more video content from a brand or business they support.[110]

- 86% of marketing professionals use video as a marketing tool.[111]

- Even today in Web3, video still dominates. However, new technology is quickly opening new worlds—literally.

Web3: Gaming Engines

Historically, Hollywood has led the way in terms of video technology, but in Web3, this truth flips upside down. Headlines tell a powerful story of how video game engines are the new kid on the block, reshaping the way we think about digital imagery. Here are three such headlines:

- Game engines are changing Hollywood's power structure.[112]

- The Birth of New Hollywood—The Game Engine Revolution.[113]

- Lights, camera, graphics: How Epic helps Hollywood.[114]

Video Game Engine companies like Unreal and Unity now influence everything digital, including movies and television series. The Mandalorian, a television series based upon the Star Wars franchise, was shot on a holodeck-esque set with Unreal Engine. One publication wrote that "this video depicts one of the most radical evolutions of filmmaking in years."

Viewers seemed to agree. It was nominated for Outstanding Drama Series at the 72nd Primetime Emmy Awards and won seven Primetime Creative Arts Emmy Awards.

This major shift is occurring in real time. These are the same Engines creating metaverses like Fortnite. Futurists see where this is all pointing:

> Instead of thinking of the Open Metaverse as a video game, think of it as a digital Gamespace. You're not just playing; you're adding a digital layer to your physical existence. The Open Metaverse extends your day-to-day life into a new gamified frontier, where you can chase professional and financial opportunities, experience love and heartbreak, freely express yourself, own your digital life, and, ultimately, craft your own story.[115]

The cutting-edge technology provided by Game Engines will pave the way for what I call The Great Metagration™. In this new embodied Internet, we're blending physical and digital reality with real and virtual worlds.

Lines blur. Realities merge. And life is changed—forever.

Game Engines play an important role, making these new worlds believable and engaging. "Web3 is the future," said Michael Shaulov, CEO of Fireblocks, adding that "we've already entered a new era of the Internet."[116]

Bonus Video

INTELLECTUAL PROPERTY

	Web 1 1991-2004	Web 2 2004-2021	Web 3 2022-?
Intellectual Property	Copyright/ Tradmark Patent	Digital Sigature	Easy IP™

Before we dive into Intellectual Property, you might want to know why. A word of warning, skipping this section might cost you millions of dollars—literally. This is because in Web3, most of the value of people's businesses, books, and brands are represented in intangible assets (Intellectual Property), not in tangible assets.

Thanks to my incredibly smart lawyer friends Keegan Caldwell and Katherine Ann Rubino, I've learned because of new data and special programs, entrepreneurs, creators, and business owners can borrow up to 50% of the value of their Intellectual Property. (For more on this topic, I highly recommend reaching out to Caldwell IP, the fastest-growing IP Law Firm many years in a row. You can find them at Caldwellip.com)

I met Keegan through Dan Sullivan at Strategic Coach™. After hearing him speak, I immediately resonated with his view of Intellectual Property. After doing research on him and his firm, I became a client. At the two companies I founded, Igniting Souls and Blockchain Life, we publish and protect IP. We're committed to helping authors, entrepreneurs, and influencers leverage their assets and reap all the benefits, up to eighteen streams of income for their book-based businesses.

Here's the quick backstory on Intellectual Property and why I believe it's one of the most exciting components of Web3.

In 1975, only 17% of the S&P 500 were intangible assets (Intellectual Property). If you're not familiar with the S&P 500, it's the stock market index tracking the stock performance of 500 large companies listed on exchanges in the United States. It's also one of the most commonly followed equity indices.[117]

Simply put, before Web1, most of the assets for the best-performing companies were tangible assets like land, buildings, equipment, cash, bonds, and inventory.

Thanks to the Internet, these statistics shifted. In 2020, for the first time, 90% of assets in the S&P 500 were intangible assets like patents, technology, software, customer data, and branding.[118]

As we've learned throughout this book, the current digital age favors a Creator Economy. This means the most value related to your business is your Intellectual Property.

Let's unpack how each version of the Internet protects Intellectual Property differently.

Web 1: Copyright / Trademark / Patent

Nobody wants to create something only to have it stolen by copycats. For this reason, historically there are three main legal shields to protect your intellectual property: copyrights, trademarks, and patents. Here's a quick summary:[119]

Copyrights: Protects "original works of authorship," such as writings, art, architecture, and music.

Trademarks: A word, symbol, design, or phrase that denotes a specific product and differentiates it from similar products. Brand names and corporate logos are primary examples. A service mark is similar, except that it safeguards the provider of a service instead of a tangible good.

Patents: Safeguards an original invention for a certain period of time and is granted by the United States Patent and Trademark Office (USPTO). By granting the right to produce a product without fear of competition for the duration of the patent, an incentive is provided for companies or individuals to continue developing innovative new products or services.

In the world of Intellectual Property, the above definitions are too simple. Of course, there are nuances and also the reason why oftentimes we need lawyers to interpret the law. Notice these important distinctions below.[120]

Copyrights:

1. Unregistered Copyrights: A copyright is the right to make copies of, license others to make copies of, or otherwise use an artistic or creative work. Copyrights protect how something is expressed rather than a specific good or fact. It's exclusive, meaning only one entity can hold the copyright and use the copyrighted material. The range of things that can be copyrighted is long and includes literary works, music, sound recordings, movies, photography, and art.

   Unlike the ten-year limit a registered trademark carries, a copyright lasts for the lifetime of the creator plus seventy years after they die. Creators also aren't required to file for official registration with the government. According to the US Copyright Office, eligible published and unpublished works are protected "the moment it is created and fixed in a tangible form."

2. Registered Copyrights: You must register with the copyright office if you want to take someone to court for copyright infringement, however.

Trademarks:

1. Unregistered Trademark: Using the trademark superscript could mean that the claimed product is in the process of registering for a government-registered trademark.

2. Registered Trademark: The ® on a product means that it's a registered trademark, meaning the brand name or logo is protected by (officially registered in) the US Patent and Trademark Office, while plain old ™

trademarks have no legal backing. Note that a trademark prohibits any marks that have a "likelihood of confusion" with an existing one.

3. Protections for registered trademarks last for ten years and can be renewed after that. If a person or business uses the registered name, logo, or symbol without prior approval from the person who owns the trademark, they can be taken to court for trademark infringement.

Patents:

There are three types of patents

1. **Utility Patents:** A utility patent covers the creation of a new or improved product, process, or machine. Also known as a "patent for invention," it bars other individuals or companies from making, using, or selling the creation without consent. Utility patents are good for up to twenty years after the patent application is filed but require the holder to pay regularly scheduled maintenance fees.

2. **Plant Patents:** A plant patent protects a new and unique plant's key characteristics from being copied, sold, or used by others. It is also good for twenty years after the application is filed.

3. **Design Patents:** A design patent applies to the unique look of a manufactured item. Take, for example, an automobile with a distinctive hood or headlight shape. These visual elements are part of the car's identity and may add to its value; however, without protecting these components with a patent, competitors could potentially copy them without legal consequences.[121]

Web2: Digital Signature

Chances are you've signed a legal document or two through a digital signature. Medical records, business contracts, and release forms are all examples of documents that integrate digital signatures. Businesses that don't offer this option are considered archaic and inefficient. Soon, such businesses may no longer be in business.

Many providers offer digital signature services. DocuSign, one such company, does a brilliant job of explaining digital signatures:

> Digital signatures are like electronic "fingerprints." In the form of a coded message, the digital signature securely associates a signer with a document in a recorded transaction. Digital signatures use a standard, accepted format, called Public Key Infrastructure (PKI), to provide the highest levels of security and universal acceptance. They are a specific signature technology implementation of electronic signature (eSignature).[122]

Web3: Easy IP™

Copyrights, trademarks, and patents aren't going anywhere, anytime soon. However, a new capability is now possible with Web3, one that's faster, cheaper, and easier.

As an author and publisher, I see the world through the lens of books. Immediately, I realized how NFTs could forever change the book publishing industry and Intellectual Property in general.

Unfortunately, most authors, entrepreneurs, and influencers don't understand the value of their Intellectual Property. Most don't know how to leverage it either. As a result, they never fully optimize their influence, impact, and income. I never felt right about this fact, and I knew I needed to do something about it.

Don't misunderstand. Patents have their place. But it's similar to bringing a nuclear weapon to a knife fight. You're going to win.

However, patents require quite a bit of time (average of three years) and they take quite a bit of money ($15,000 or more).

As a result, most people can't afford to file patents. Besides, unless you're planning on selling your company or borrowing money from the patent valuation, then securing a patent is probably overkill. Also, it doesn't help that eighty-six percent of patents get rejected by the USPTO.[123]

This is where Easy IP™ comes in. By leveraging blockchain technology and the power of smart contracts and NFTs, we've developed a patent-pending capability that protects Intellectual Property.

Notice I said, patent pending. This is because some-day I may sell the technology (Easy IP™) and the company (Blockchain Life). As a result, I wanted to protect this Intellectual Property with "the nuclear weapon."

Guess who I hired to help with this one expression of Intellectual Property? Caldwell IP.

However, as an author and entrepreneur, there's no way I'm going to file patents on all my Intellectual Property. I have thousands of expressions of IP, and doing so would require millions and millions of dollars. Not only is this impractical, but it's also unnecessary.

Rather than securing patents, I'm protecting all of my other Intellectual Property with EasyIP™. Although all the details can be found at EasyIP.today, here's a quick peek:

Who: Authors, entrepreneurs, influencers, businesses, brands, and organizations.

What: Intellectual Property protection through proprietary technology and smart contracts.

When: Real-time Intellectual Property protection.

Where: A public blockchain with low gas fees, high speeds, robust security.

Why: Intellectual Property protection that's cheaper, faster, easier.

IP Protection	Average Cost*	Average Time
Patent	*$15,000*	*3 Years*
Easy IP™	*$100*	*24 Hours*

* Average costs are estimates. Pricing can fluctuate based upon packages.

Easy IP™ is the Intellectual Property solution for this new world. Humanity has officially moved into Web3, the "new version of the Internet."

Through our proprietary patent-pending process, Easy IP™ integrates blockchain technology to give your Intellectual Property "global protection." By creating a "time-stamped" smart contract that can never be tampered with or changed, we establish a "first use case" that tracks back to you, the owner.

The result is IP protection that's faster, cheaper, and easier.

Experts believe that soon all transactions will be done via smart contracts, including marriage licenses, real estate deeds, vehicle titles, academic diplomas, and business agreements.

Smart contracts are the way of the future. Currently, states and countries recognize this technology in a court of law. Smart contracts are quickly becoming the preferred medium for several reasons:[124]

1. Accuracy

2. Transparency

3. Autonomy

4. Speed

5. Communication

6. Efficiency

7. Paper-free

8. Trust

9. Savings

10. Backup

11. Cost reduction

12. Automatic updates

None of this technology would have been possible without Web3. Easy IP™ is just one more example of how the new version of the Internet opens doors for new innovation and capabilities.

Bonus Video

LEGAL

	Web 1 1991-2004	Web 2 2004-2021	Web 3 2022-?
Legal	Physical Contract	Digital Contract	Smart Contract

Contracts are the foundation for all commerce and human relationships. Everything from mailing a stamp to getting married relies upon contracts. Thanks to the Internet, contracts have been reimagined.

Web 1: Physical Contract

Physical contracts have existed since the beginning of human history. According to the Biblical tradition, God made a physical contract with Adam back in the Garden of Eden. Throughout the centuries, a handshake signified a physical contract.

Physical contracts were the only type of contract until 1867, when US courts debated the validity of an electronic signature transmitted via telegraph.[125] Despite the emergence of new technologies over the past 150 years, physical contracts still remained the preferred vehicle throughout Web1.

Web2: Digital Contract

As people became more comfortable with the Internet, fears of digital contracts subsided. Today, many of us sign digital contracts on a daily basis in places like smoothie shops, gas stations, and doctor offices. This is due to the laws that passed in late Web1.

The ESIGN Act, a federal law passed in 2000, granted legal recognition to electronic signatures and records if all parties to a contract choose to use electronic documents and to sign them electronically.

DigiSigner believes traditional signatures will soon become outdated. Electronic signatures are simpler and easier to use, plus they are legally binding.[126]

Web3: Smart Contract

Smart contracts rely on several Web3 components, including blockchain technology. They're computer programs stored on a blockchain that run when predetermined conditions are met. As we learned, blockchain technology allows continuously growing records, enabling verification of transactions that are trackable and immutable.

Smart contracts are used to automate the execution of an agreement so that all participants can be immediately certain of the outcome, without any intermediary's involvement or time loss. They can also automate a workflow, triggering the next action when conditions are met.[127]

Bonus Video

LOGIN

	Web 1 1991-2004	Web 2 2004-2021	Web 3 2022- ?
Login	Username/ Password	Social	Web3 Wallet

Leveraging the Internet requires connecting to the Internet. Each version of the Internet utilizes a different way of logging on.

Web 1: Username/Password

Most platforms within Web1 required a username and password login. If you've ever "logged" into a platform, you know the experience. "User authentication" has three tasks:

1. Manage the connection between the human (user) and the website's server (computer).

2. Verify users' identities.

3. Approve (or decline) the authentication so the system can move to authorizing the user.

Many Web1 advocates store their usernames and passwords on notebooks or scrap paper. Just ask your friend. This habit causes most cybersecurity experts to shake in their shoes. It's clear we needed a better way than this Web1 technology.

Web2: Social

"Please don't open any messages from me. My account has been hacked."

If you've ever used social media you've probably seen this post. Few experiences cause the same amount of alarm you feel when your account is hacked. This is one of the reasons why you wouldn't want to use a "social login."

If you're unfamiliar with social logins, they're quite simple and common. Rather than people signing in to a website with a username and password, they sign in using their Facebook, LinkedIn, or other social media account. Social media integration creates a seamless user experience that increases convenience and satisfaction. Eliminating the need for users to keep track of multiple usernames and passwords results in higher visits to a website or platform.[128]

An article published back in 2014—the height of Web2—provided compelling statistics on why businesses should shift from username and password logins to social logins. The author Oliver McGough raises some interesting points in his article titled, "Should we be using Social Logins over the traditional process?"

In his article, he shared positive results. "Not only do 65% prefer social logins, but 60% believe that companies offering social logging are more up to date and innovative; not only do they benefit the user, they benefit your brand."

But he also gave negative results with a MailChimp case study. "Insights showed that just 3.4% of users actually made use of MailChimp's new social logins. On top of this, their CEO declared that he felt the logins cheapened the experience, devaluing the brand and cluttering the page by using Facebook and Twitter buttons."

The biggest concern is the question over ownership. A social login muddies the waters.

Who does the account belong to?

And what happens if the social platform goes under?

Most people didn't bother to question ownership. We just checked the box on the fine print and agreed to give up all our rights so we could use the social media platforms.

Back in 2014, we didn't quite understand data mining or privacy issues. Web2 hadn't witnessed Mark Zuckerberg's testimony on Capitol Hill. That would come four years later.

Web3: Web3 Wallet

Web3 offers a new type of login, the most popular being Web3 Wallets. In one sense, Web3 Wallets are digital wallets. In another sense, they're much more.

Here's the difference:

Digital Wallet

- Apple Cash: Built right into the iPhone, making it an easy way to send and receive money. And because it's a digital card that lives in Wallet, your Apple

Cash can be spent in stores, online, and in apps with Apple Pay.[129]

- Apple Pay: The safe way to pay and make secure purchases in stores, in apps, and on the web.[130]

- Apple Wallet: An app on iPhone and Apple Watch that securely and conveniently organizes your credit and debit cards, transit passes, boarding passes, tickets, identity cards, keys, rewards cards, and more—all in one place.[131]

All of the examples above run without blockchain technology. Therefore, they're classified as Web2 tools.

Web3 Wallets are different because they leverage blockchain technology. These three popular ones below highlight different benefits:

Web3 Wallet

- Coinbase Wallet: Store all of your crypto and NFTs in one place. Explore the decentralized web on your phone or browser.[132]

- MetaMask: A crypto wallet and gateway to blockchain apps.[133]

- Trust Wallet: Buy, store, collect NFTs, exchange and earn crypto. Browser for dApps.[134]

Web3 wallets are magical. You can connect to all dApps (Decentralized Apps) with a crypto wallet."[135] "They also have the ability to store digital assets, including everything from fungible to non-fungible (NFTs) tokens. Web3 wallets also open the door to the crypto realm, allowing you to interact with various blockchains."[136]

One of the coolest features is that when you visit the Internet, thanks to a browser extension, your Web3 Wallet goes with you wherever you go. Extensions add features and functions to a browser. This means everything in your wallet goes with you, too, including digital assets.

Think back to our section on NFTs. One day in the near future, all your information—medical records, investments, certificates, Intellectual Property—will be expressed in the form of digital assets. These will travel with you across the Internet, making it incredibly easy to not only log in, but when you do, all your most important and relevant assets will be there for you to use. This could include digital art, clothes, purchases, mortgages, vehicle titles, past tickets to concerts, games, shows, and more.

Bonus Video

REALITY

	Web 1 1991-2004	Web 2 2004-2021	Web 3 2022- ?
Reality	Physical Reality	Augmented Reality	Mixed Reality

Throughout history, philosophers explored questions surrounding reality.

Plato said, "Reality is created by the mind. We can change our reality by changing our mind." More than a thousand years later, René Descartes declared, "I think, therefore I am." And a few decades ago, Morpheus asked Neo, "Do you think that's air you're breathing now?"

Each generation questioned reality, but in a different way. With the rise of the Internet, reality became even more complex to comprehend.

Web 1: Physical Reality

I remember going to the mall with my friends back in the nineties to frequent the arcade. On one particular visit, in the middle of the mall, a virtual reality station set up shop. We watched our friend Joel strap on the headset.

He flailed his arms around fighting something: ghosts, monsters, villains. Who knows? We couldn't see his reality, and he was ignorant of ours. When he took off the headset, we clearly saw he traveled somewhere—we just didn't know where. It took a moment for him to get reoriented.

Despite this advance in technology, his virtual reality experience had massive limitations. It was solo gameplay, disconnected from the Internet. There was little integration between real life and digital life.

Bottom line, in spite of a bulky headset, in Web 1, physical reality still reigned supreme for the majority of people.

Web2: Augmented Reality

In the 2002 film Minority Report, Tom Cruise and Steven Spielberg gave us a peek into the future. The film is set in Washington, D.C., and northern Virginia in the year 2054, where Precrime, a specialized police department, apprehends criminals based on foreknowledge provided by three psychics called "precogs."[137]

During the making of the film, the producers invited technology experts to provide consulting on future innovation. Gesture-based touchscreen interface, robotic surveillance, self-driving cars, and targeted ads all made the list. Many of these inventions now intersect our daily lives, including augmented reality (AR).

Augmented reality is an interactive experience of a real-world environment where the objects that reside in the real world are enhanced by computer-generated perceptual information, sometimes across multiple sensory modalities, including visual, auditory, haptic, somatosensory, and olfactory. Every year since the release of Minority Report, AR gained more and more popularity.

In 2016, all this changed, with a mobile game that turned augmented reality into a global phenomenon. *The New York Times'* headline delivered the news: "Pokémon Go Brings Augmented Reality to a Mass Audience."[138] The article introduced the concept of AR to many readers:

> AR fuses digital technology with the physical world. The idea behind the technology is to overlay digital imagery on a person's view of the real world, using a smartphone screen or a headset. Players traverse the physical world following a digital map, searching for cartoon creatures that surface at random. People look through their smartphone cameras to find Pokémon. When an animated creature appears, they toss Pokéballs at it until it is subdued.

But AR isn't just for gaming. Many companies leverage this technology to make better products and services. "Industrial augmented reality offers a better way to create and deliver easily consumable work instructions by overlaying digital content onto real-world work environments."[139]

Web3: Mixed Reality

Research the history of virtual reality and augmented reality, and you'll usually find 1968 as the date where it all began.

In this year, Ivan Sutherland and his student Bob Sproull created the first VR / AR head-mounted display (Sword of Damocles) that was connected to a computer and not a camera. The computer-generated graphics were very primitive wireframe rooms and objects.[140] In 1990, after more than two decades, Boeing researcher Tim Codell coined the term "augmented reality."[141] Obviously, this first headset didn't integrate the Internet. Just because the technology existed, it took many more decades before mass adoption.

In Web3, the latest version of the Internet, VR, and AR combine to create Mixed Reality (XR). According to *XR Today*:

> Mixed reality exists in the middle of the immersive media spectrum. On one side, you have virtual reality, which completely replaces your existing environment with a new, computerized space. On the other side, there's augmented reality, which overlays digital content into a real environment.
>
> Mixed reality blends elements of both AR and VR, to give a unique experience. Unlike AR solutions which often allow you to see digital content through a filter or app, MR allows interaction with the digital content in your space. You could use gestures to move a piece of digital content around on a virtual whiteboard and see digital avatars of your colleagues sitting beside you. Mixed Reality even has the potential to open the door for things like holograms and holoportation.[142]

Because Mixed Reality is so new, we have yet to see its full potential. As Web3 components continue integrating with each other, more and more capabilities will be created.

Most experts predict a day coming when we will never go offline. Instead, all realities will integrate into one seamless existence at all times.

Bonus Video

TECHNOLOGY

	Web 1 1991-2004	Web 2 2004-2021	Web 3 2022- ?
Technology	No Blockchain	Private Blockchain	Public Blockchain

Ask insiders about blockchain technology, and you might have this experience.

Their eyes light up.

Their speech hurries.

Their palms sweat.

And they say phrases like "this technology will change the world!"

Are they being melodramatic, or is there something they know that most of the population doesn't? We're talking about a digital ledger, not a sports car.

What gives?

Turns out, everything. Here's a peek inside a technology that could change the way we do life and work.

Blockchains are publicly distributed ledgers typically managed by a peer-to-peer network. Nodes communicate and validate new blocks or records. Utilizing cryptography, these blocks are linked with a cryptographic hash of the previous block. This creates a timestamp for anyone and everyone to see. These blocks form a chain, with each additional block reinforcing the ones before it.

Blockchains are immutable (unchanging), because once recorded, the data in any given block cannot be altered without altering all subsequent blocks. This is made possible because the blockchain is decentralized, meaning no one person or organization controls it.

Bottom line, blockchain is a transparent world where trust abounds. It makes new things possible. Friction-free. Decentralized. Permissionless. Immutable. Global.

This technology might just be as exciting as insiders claim and in a moment, we'll unpack some practical applications.

Web 1: No Blockchain

Research the history of blockchain, and you'll keep stumbling upon October 31, 2008. On this day, Satoshi Nakamoto published a white paper describing a digital cryptocurrency titled, "Bitcoin: A Peer-to-Peer Electronic Cash System."

The origin story of Bitcoin reads much like a mystery, including the cloud of secrecy surrounding its creator, Satoshi Nakamoto. To this day, the identity of the pseudonym Nakamoto is not publicly known. He, she, it, or they are accredited as the brains behind Bitcoin, arguably the most popular application of this digital ledger technology.

On Saturday, January 3, 2009, Bitcoin was born. With the creation of the very first Bitcoin block—known as the "Genesis Block"—the first set of 50 BTC was mined into existence. Embedded in the coinbase transaction of this block is the text: *The Times 03/Jan/2009 Chancellor on brink of second bailout for banks*, citing a headline in the UK newspaper The Times published on that date.[143]

According to *Decrypt*, because of the timing of its release, in addition to the hidden message contained in the genesis block, it is widely believed that Bitcoin was released to provide an alternative monetary system designed to resist the challenges faced by many traditional currencies—like inflation, counterfeiting, and corruption.[144]

Many people new to blockchain assume it's the same thing as cryptocurrency. This isn't true. Currencies may function on the blockchain ledger, but they are not the blockchain.

Blockchain technology is older than Bitcoin, more than fifteen years older. In 1991, research scientists Stuart Haber and W. Scott Stornetta set out to introduce a computationally practical solution for time-stamping digital documents so they could not be backdated or tampered. They developed a system using the concept of a cryptographically secured chain of blocks to store the time-stamped documents.[145]

In 1992, they incorporated a data structure used in computer science applications called Merkle Tree to make blockchain more efficient by allowing several documents to be collected into one block.[146] Thanks to Ralph Merkle, who described an approach to public key distribution and digital signatures called "tree authentication" in his 1979 Ph.D. thesis for Stanford University, he eventually patented this idea as a method for providing digital signatures. The Merkle Tree provides a data structure for verifying individual records and was a key component to the creation of blockchain technology.[147]

More than a decade after Haber and Stornetta's initial idea, in 2004, computer scientist and cryptographic activist Hal Finney introduced a system called Reusable Proof of Work(RPoW) as a prototype for digital cash. This essential and early step in the history of cryptocurrencies solved the double-spending problem by keeping the ownership of tokens registered on a trusted server. RPoW allowed users throughout the world to verify its correctness and integrity in real time.[148]

Despite their efforts, blockchain technology wasn't adopted in Web1. However, the stage was set for blockchain technology to gain traction in Web2.

Web2: Private Blockchain

Initially, private blockchains took center stage. In this scenario, only a single authority or organization had control over the network. Also called permissioned blockchains, users needed approval before being permitted to participate in the system making transactions or validating and authenticating blockchain changes.

Private blockchains are not decentralized, but instead, they operate as a closed database secured by cryptography. This essential feature protects confidential information such as supply, logistics, payroll, finances, and accounting.[149]

Not everyone is a fan of private blockchains, especially the Web3 faithful who favor public blockchains.

Web3: Public Blockchain

Public blockchains are permissionless blockchains because they don't require permission to join or use. Blockchain purists often despise private blockchains, arguing such networks are not real blockchains.

They have a point.

Remember the definition of a blockchain:

A blockchain is a time-stamped decentralized series of fixed records that contains data of any size controlled by a large network of computers that are scattered around the globe and not owned by a single organization. Every block is secured and connected with each other using hashing technology which protects it from being tampered by an unauthorized person.[150]

According to Geeks for Geeks, true blockchains contain seven characteristics.

1. **Immutable:** They are permanent and unalterable networks.

2. **Distributed:** All network participants have a copy of the ledger for complete transparency.

3. **Decentralized:** There is no central governing authority responsible for all the decisions.

4. **Secure:** All the records in the blockchain are individually encrypted.

5. **Consensus:** Uses consensus, a decision-making algorithm, to help the network make quick and unbiased decisions.

6. **Unanimous:** All the network participants agree to the validity of the records before they can be added to the network.

7. **Faster Settlement:** Offers a faster settlement compared to traditional banking systems.

Other publications suggest even more benefits, including better capacity, no intermediaries, and greater security due to no single point of failure.

Since many of these characteristics aren't found in private blockchains, Web3 purists reject private blockchains.

On the flip side, thanks to open-source thinking, public blockchains have been gaining popularity, and for good reason. The use cases for public blockchains increase on a daily basis, due to the decentralized and trustless components of this technology.

Bonus Video

VENUE

	Web 1 1991-2004	Web 2 2004-2021	Web 3 2022- ?
Venue	Sites	Platforms	Metaverses

Internet venues have shifted throughout the decades, but their importance hasn't. We've engaged the Internet in different ways, expecting different outcomes.

Web 1: Sites

In Web1, we visited sites. These websites contained web pages that provided information. The Internet was a collection of static independent pieces, together making up the whole.

Web2: Platforms

In Web2 we participated on platforms. We entered Facebook, LinkedIn, and YouTube, and we could stay for days—literally. This dynamic Internet captured our attention and profited from our data.

Web3: Metaverse

In Web3, we experience metaverses.

And what exactly is the metaverse? Sometimes new words are confusing. Matthew Ball, author of Metaverse, defines the metaverse as:

> A massively scaled and interoperable network of real- time rendered 3D virtual worlds that can be experienced syn- chronously and persistently by an effectively unlimited number of users with an individual sense of presence, and with continuity of data, such as identity, history, entitlements, objects, communications, and payments.[151]

I suggest a simpler definition. The metaverse is an embod- ied Internet where we blend physical and digital reality with real and virtual worlds.

No one can deny our worlds converged—physical and digital—hence the new word phygital, meaning a fusion of the words physical and digital. We find ourselves right in the middle of The Great Metagration™.

Some think the metaverse isn't here—or Web3 for that matter. Really?

Technological revolutions rarely come with an announce- ment or a global event. Historians like to point back and connect the dots, but it's never black and white.

Metaverses range from meetings on Zoom to concerts in Decentraland. We can enter metaverses as ourselves or our avatars. We engage via screens on our phones or virtual reality goggles on our heads. Options expand every day, and they won't stop. The tipping point will be interoperability—the ability to unify economies, avatars, and systems across worlds.[152]

Today, many people already live and work within the metaverse. Before we cast the stone of judgment, consider the average senior citizen. Adults over age sixty-five spent almost three times more of their waking hours watching TV than younger adults.[153] "Among seniors, we have issues of isolation, undiagnosed and untreated depression, and loneliness," said Dr. Martin Gorbien, director of geriatric medicine and palliative care at Rush University Medical Center in Chicago.

In the metaverse, senior citizens don't sit and stagnate. Rather, they can exercise with friends or travel to different virtual countries. Instead of rejecting the technology, maybe we should rethink the technology.

Avoid the harmful. Appropriate the beneficial.

Dissecting this book might be your first step. Choosing how you show up in Web3 is your next step and the final section.

Bonus Video

PART 3
CREATION

IDENTITY

Technology is a target—innovation always has been and always will be. But before we boycott Web3 or buy into it, we must seek to understand it and dissect the hype from the hope.

The Internet isn't only a topic we discuss. It's a technology shaping the way we think and act. Most of us don't live a day without it.

This technology influences our health, finances, faith, work, and education.

Now comes the most exciting question. How will you show up in Web3? You only have three choices: critic, consumer, or creator.

1. Critic: You criticize Web3

2. Consumer: You consume Web3

3. Creator: You create Web3

Which will you choose? I don't know about you, but I'm choosing #3, Creator.

Rather than getting overwhelmed and trying to do all the components on the Web Comparison Chart™, my advice is to start by picking one area. Explore. Be a little kid again. Have fun.

Web Comparison Chart™

©2022 Kary Oberbrunner. Permission granted to use with attribution anywhere, everywhere.

	Web 1 1991-2004	**Web 2** 2004-2021	**Web 3** 2022-?
Motto	*They create.* *They own.*	*We create.* *They own.*	*We create.* *We own.*
Access	Desktop	Mobile	Wearable
Assets	Physical	Digital	NFTs
Benefit	Informational	Social	Experiential
Byproduct	Information Gathering	Data Mining	Open Source
Component	Advertising	Algorithms	Artificial Intelligence
Control	Decentralized	Centralized	Decentralized
Currency	Credit Cards	Payment Aggregators	Cryptocurrencies
Danger	Phishing	Hacking	Deepfaking
Economy	Information	Attention	Creator
Experience	Static	Dynamic	Interactive
Extreme	Dot-Com Bubble	*The Social Dilemma*	Transhumanism
Function	Reading	Writing	Executing
Governance	Individuals	Big Tech	DAOs
Image	Clip Art	Videos	Gaming Engines
Intellectual Property	Copyright / Trademark Patent	Digital Signature	Easy IP™
Legal	Physical Contract	Digital Contract	Smart Contract
Login	Username / Password	Social	Web3 Wallet
Reality	Physical Reality	Augmented Reality	Mixed Reality
Technology	No Blockchain	Private Blockchain	Public Blockchain
Venue	Sites	Platforms	Metaverses

Once you get familiar, then you can dive deeper. Eventually, you'll gain confidence and competence. Who knows, you might even develop mastery in an area. This was my path and Lee's path too.

What about Web2.5?

There's a phrase floating out there and I must admit, I kind of like it. Web2.5 will soon be our experience.

Here's why. People rarely go from Web2 to Web3 in a simple manner. It's never a clean break. Quite the opposite. It's often messy, clunky, and less than ideal. In a few short months many people will wake up in Web2.5, caught somewhere between two worlds.

Lee and I chatted yesterday on this topic. She used a great analogy, saying people will travel from Web2 to Web3 via tunnel or via bridge. She's right.

- Tunnels are covert and unconscious.
- Bridges are overt and conscious.

Starbucks knows this too and so they've chosen a tunnel. Caffeine-savvy customers will soon experience Web3 unintentionally.

Starbucks went public with their desire of onboarding patrons into Web3 without the friction of digital wallets and blockchain technology. They're creating immersive coffee experiences with digital assets that grow profit by fostering customer loyalty and engagement.

This is how many will eventually end up in Web3, without even knowing.

Don't be that person

I hear a common story when people reflect back upon Web1. They say things like:

If only I bought Amazon or Apple stock when they went public. I had the same idea back in the nineties. I just never acted on it.

I wish I had jumped into Bitcoin back in the beginning.

Notice the theme with all three statements—**regret.**

Look, I don't know exactly what you're supposed to do personally or professionally with Web3. Anyone who says they do is probably trying to sell you something.

What I do know is that you can't ignore Web3. One day in the near future, people will look back on Web3 and wish they would have taken action.

Don't wish. You have the power of this present moment.

As a CEO of a writing, publishing, and marketing agency I know I can't just sit on the sidelines while Web3 keeps expanding. If I want to stay relevant, I must get in the game and stay in the game. This is why last year, after understanding the potential of these new technologies, we filmed a course in Virtual Reality called Write Your Book. We partnered with a Phoenix based company called Genius X and leveraged their app RetreatVR.io The developers designed a brand new world where I teach aspiring authors how to write their book all through an immersive experience.

Why? For starters, the science of VR is hard to debate:

- 4x faster to train then in the classroom

- 275% more confident to apply skills after training

- 3.75x more emotionally connected to content than in the classroom

- 4x more focused than e-learning peers

Bottom line, my writing students get a better, faster, and easier experience.

If you need help, entering into this brand new world of Web3 please reach out to Lee or myself. We've both created simple and powerful resources to help you along the way. We're passionate about this topic and we love to equip individuals and organizations with customized strategies to reimagine who they want to be in this exciting new digital world.

Thanks for joining us on this journey.

It's truly an exciting time to be alive—in real life and in the metaverse.

Bonus Video

ENDNOTES

1   Mark Spoonauer. "This 12-year-old has made nearly $6 million with NFTs—and she's just getting started." Tom's Guide. December 28, 2021. https://www.tomsguide. com/news/this-12-year-old-has-made-nearly-dollar6-million-with-nfts-and-shes-just-getting-started.

2   Life.Church. "Life.Church in the Metaverse." Accessed September 25, 2022. https://www.life.church/metaverse/.

3   Adam Brown. "Crypto Investors Wanted To Buy The Constitution. Instead, They Birthed Another Hyped-Up Meme Coin." Forbes. December 1, 2021. https://www.forbes.com/sites/abrambrown/2021/12/01/crypto-tokens-people-constitution-dao-ether-redeem-refund/?sh=326250906f3f.

4   CryptoCom. "Fortune Favours the Brave." October 28, 2021. YouTube Video, 1:00. https://www.youtube.com/watch?v=9hBC5TVdYT8.

5   Pin Lean Lau. "The metaverse: three legal issues we need to address." The Conversation. February 1, 2022. https://theconversation.com/the-metaverse-three-legal-issues-we-need-to-address-175891.

6   Mike Elgan. "You can safely ignore Web3." Computerworld, December 28, 2021. https://www.computerworld.com/article/3645691/you-can-safely-ignore-web3.html.

7   Jenny List. "Unpicking The Hype Around Web 3, What's The Tech?" Hackaday. January 20, 2022. https://hackaday.com/2022/01/20/unpicking-the-hype-around-web-3-whats-the-tech/.

8   Denise Fournier, Ph.D. "The Only Way to Eat an Elephant." Psychology Today. April 24, 2018. https://www.psychologytoday.com/us/blog/mindfully-present-fully-alive/201804/the-only-way-eat-elephant.

9   Mark Zuckerberg. "Founder's Letter, 2021." Meta. October 28, 2021. https://about.fb.com/news/2021/10/founders-letter/.

10   Douglas Rushkoff. *Present Shock*. New York: Current, 2014.

11   RR Auction®. "How do you show provenance?" September 20, 2017. https://rrauctionsellconsignments.com/how-do-you-show-prove-nance/.

12   terminalfour. "Fad or future: Can NFTs transform higher education?" July 27, 2022. https://www.terminalfour.com/blog/posts/fad-or-future-can-nfts-transform-higher-education.html.

13   Vignesh Karunanidhi. "South Korean University Will Issue NFT Degrees To All 2830 Graduates." Tron Weekly. February 19, 2022. https://www.tronweekly.com/south-korean-university-issue-nft-to-graduates/.

14   Ibid.

15   Evan Andrews. "8 Legendary Ancient Libraries." History. com. August 22, 2018. https://www.history.com/news/ 8-impressive-ancient-libraries.

16   Science and Media Museum. "A short history of the internet." December 3, 2020. https://www. scienceandmediamuseum.org.uk/objects-and-stories/ short-history-internet.

17   Yevgeniy Sverdlik. "Web3 Builders Hope to Fix Open Source, 'Broken' by Web 2.0." Equinix Metal. September 30, 2021. https://metal.equinix.com/blog/ web3-and-open-source/.

18   Teads. "20 years since the first banner ad—what can we learn from it today?" October 31, 2014. https://www.teads. com/2014-10-20-years-since-the-first-banner-ad-what- can-we-learn-from-it-t/.

19   Matthew Caines. "'You are more likely to summit Mount Everest than click on a banner ad.'" The Guardian. October 23, 2013. https://www.theguardian.com/ media-network/media-network-blog/2013/oct/23/ buzzfeed-jonathan-perel-man-ad-banner.

20   NBC News. "Pop-Up Ads Creator Ethan Zuckerman: 'I'm Sorry.'" August 15, 2014. https://www.nbcnews.com/tech/ tech-news/pop-up-ads-creator-ethan-zuckerman-im- sorry-n182096.

21   Brent Barnhart. "Everything You Need to Know About Social Media Algorithms." March 26, 2021. https:// sproutsocial.com/insights/social-media-algorithms/.

22   Dictionary.com. "Artificial intelligence Definition & Meaning." Accessed September 25, 2022. https://www. dictionary.com/browse/artificial-intelligence.

23   Rebecca Reynoso. "A Complete History of Artificial Intelligence." G2. May 25, 2021. https://www.g2.com/ articles/history-of-artificial-intelligence.

24   Bernard Marr. "13 Mind-Blowing Things Artificial Intelligence Can Already Do Today." Forbes. November 11, 2019. https://www.forbes.com/sites/bernard-marr/2019/11/11/13-mind-blowing-things-artificial-intelligence-can-already-do-to-day/?sh=8630c5765020.

25   Ed Newton-Rex. "59 Impressive Things Artificial Intelligence Can Do Today." Insider. March 7, 2017. https://www.businessinsider.com/artificial-intelligence-ai-most-impressive-achievements-2017-3#what-ai-cando-everyday-human-stuff-1.

26   Kai-Fu Lee & Chen Qiufan. "What AI cannot do." Big Think. January 19, 2022. https://bigthink.com/the-future/what-ai-cannot-do/.

27   Rob Toews. "What Artificial Intelligence Still Can't Do." Forbes. June 1, 2021. https://www.forbes.com/sites/robtoews/2021/06/01/what-artificial-intelligence-still-cant-do/?sh=3b43c71b66f6

28   Jeff Wong. "Cutting Through The Web3 Hype: AI In The Decentralized Web." Forbes. August 4, 2022. https://www.forbes.com/sites/forbestechcoun-cil/2022/08/04/cutting-through-the-web3-hype-ai-in-the-decentralized-web/?sh=-5ca4752c52ee.

29   Ibid.

30   Jesus Rodriguez. "Web 3's Use of AI Will Present Challenges, but They Are Not Insurmountable." Coindesk. March 14, 2022. https://www.coindesk.com/layer2/2022/03/14/web-3s-use-of-ai-will-present-challenges-but-they-are-not-insur-mountable/.

31   Rand Hindi. "In the 90s, Web 1.0 was Running on a Fully Decentralized Infrastructure." Hackernoon. November 25, 2021. https://hackernoon.com/in-the-90s-web-10-was-running-on-a-fully-decentralized-infrastructure.

32   Ibid.

33 Rand Hindi. "The Real Value of Ethereum. How Ethereum's standardization efforts created the most innovative ecosystem to date." Medium. October 30, 2021. https://medium.com/@randhindi/the-real-value-of-ethereum-741f83b0c9de.

34 Tim Ferriss (@tferriss). "'I think Web3 is not only better for the world, but it's also going to beat Web2. It's going to be more popular because the people get really excited . . .'" Twitter. October 18, 2021, 3:48 p.m. https://twitter.com/tferriss/ status/1453826030515507202?lang=en.

35 Doug Petkanics. "The Benefits of Decentralization." Medium. November 15, 2016. https://petkanics.medium.com/the-benefits-of-decentralization-88a0b5d0fd39.

36 VISA. "Visa Celebrates 25 Years of Ecommerce." April 12, 2019. https://usa.visa.com/visa-everywhere/blog/bdp/2019/08/12/visa-cele- brates-25-1565646929402.html.

37 Peter H. Lewis. "Attention Shoppers: Internet is Open." The New York Times. August 12, 1994. https://www.nytimes.com/1994/08/12/business/attention-shoppers-internet-is-open.html.

38 VISA. "Visa Celebrates 25 Years of Ecommerce."

39 Peter H. Lewis. "Attention Shoppers: Internet is Open."

40 Payments Next. "Visa's 25-year anniversary of first e-commerce payment." Accessed September 26, 2022. https://paymentsnext.com/visas-25-year-anniversary-of-first-e-commerce-payment/.

41 Square. "What is a Payment Aggregator?" Accessed September 26, 2022. https://squareup.com/au/en/townsquare/what-is-payment-aggregator.

42 Stephanie Chevalier. "Global retail e-commerce sales 2026." Statista. September 21, 2022. https://www.statista.com/statistics/379046/worldwide-retail-e-commerce-sales/.

43　Digital Commerce 360. "Global cross-border ecommerce grows 21%." Accessed September 26, 2022. https://www.digitalcommerce360.com/2020/07/28/global-cross-border-ecommerce-grows-21/.

44　Jessica Young. "US ecommerce grows 14.2% in 2021." Digital Commerce 360. February 18, 2022. https://www.digitalcommerce360.com/article/us-ecommerce-sales/.

45　Shelley E. Kohan. "Amazon's Net Profit Soars 84% With Sales Hitting $386 Billion," February 2, 2021. https://www.forbes.com/sites/shelleykohan/2021/02/02/amazons-net-profit-soars-84-with-sales-hitting-386-billion/?sh=4dde48601334.

46　Oberlo, "Mobile Commerce Sales in 2022," Accessed September 26, 2022. https://www.oberlo.com/statistics/mobile-commerce-sales.

47　Branka Vuleta, "Ecommerce Statistics 2022 Update," 99 Firms, Accessed September 26, 2022. https://99firms.com/blog/ecommerce-statistics/.

48　G. Dautovic, "40+ Astounding eCommerce Statistics (2022)," Fortunly, January 14, 2022. https://fortunly.com/statistics/ecommerce-statistics/#gref.

49　Square, "What is a Payment Aggregator?."

50　Brianna Blaney, "What is a Payment Aggregator & is It the Right Approach for Your Business?" Tipalti. Accessed September 26, 2022. https://tipalti.com/what-is-a-payment-aggregator/.

51　Merriam-Webster. "Fiat money Definition & Meaning." Accessed September 26, 2022. https://www.merriam-webster.com/dictionary/fiat%20money.

52　James Chen. "Fiat Money Definition." Investopedia. April 19, 2022. https://www.investopedia.com/terms/f/fiatmoney.asp.

53　Ibid.

54   Ibid.

55   Amanda Hetler. "How is cryptocurrency valued?"
      TechTarget. June 28, 2022. https://www.techtarget.com/
      whatis/feature/How-is-cryptocurrency-valued.

56   Trend Micro™. "Cryptocurrency—Definition." Accessed
      September 26, 2022. https://www.trendmicro.com/vinfo/
      us/security/definition/cryptocurrency.

57   Federal Reserve Bank of St. Louis. Functions of Money.
      The Economic Lowdown Podcast Series. Podcast audio.
      Accessed October 3, 2022. https://www.stlouisfed.org/
      education/economic-lowdown-podcast-series/episode-
      9-functions-of-money

58   Robert Gudmestad. "What happened to Confederate
      money after the Civil War?" Colorado State
      University. May 3, 2021. https://source.colostate.edu/
      what-happened-to-confederate-money-after-the-civil-war/.

59   Mint. "8 Pros and Cons of Bitcoin." June 30,
      2022. https://mint.intuit.com/ blog/investments/
      pros-and-cons-of-bitcoin/.

60   Phishing.org. "History of Phishing." Accessed September
      26, 2022. https:// www.phishing.org/history-of-phishing.

61   Wikipedia. "AOHell." Accessed September 26, 2022.
      https://en.wikipedia.org/wiki/AOHell.

62   Cofense. "History of Phishing." Accessed September
      26, 2022. https:// cofense.com/knowledge-center/
      history-of-phishing/.

63   Proofpoint. "What is Email Spoofing?" Accessed September
      26, 2022. https://www.proofpoint.com/us/threat-reference/
      email-spoofing.

64   Phishing.org. "History of Phishing."

65   Ibid.

66 Steve Morgan. "Cybercrime To Cost The World $10.5 Trillion Annually By 2025." Cybercrime Magazine. November 13, 2020. https://cybersecurityventures.com/hackerpocalypse-cybercrime-report-2016/.

67 Ethan Davis. "Hackers Post Deep Fake Of 2x World Champ Tom Carroll Praising Fraudulent Crypto Scheme." Stab. March 9, 2022. https://stabmag.com/elsewhere/hackers-post-deep-fake-of-2x-world-champ-tom-carroll-praising-fraudulent-crypto-scheme/.

68 Tess Bonn. "Berkeley professor warns deepfake technology being 'weaponized' against women." The Hill. July 9, 2019. https://thehill.com/hilltv/rising/452166-berkeley-professor-warns-deep-fake-technology-being-used-to-target-women/.

69 Ian Sample. "What are deepfakes—and how can you spot them?" The Guardian. January 13, 2020. https://www.theguardian.com/technology/2020/jan/13/what-are-deepfakes-and-how-can-you-spot-them.

70 Kary Oberbrunner. Unhackable. Powell, Ohio: Ethos Collective, 2020.

71 Julie Plavnik. "The creator economy: How we arrived there, and why we need its Web3 upgrade." July 16, 2022. https://cointelegraph.com/news/the-creator-economy-how-we-arrived-there-and-why-we-need-its-web3-upgrade.

72 NFT Now (@nftnow). "Swipe to learn about Web3 in 30 seconds." Instagram. July 28, 2022. https://www.instagram.com/p/CgkOGwpuIF2/.

73 Sarah Lewis. "What is interoperability?" TechTarget. Accessed September 27, 2022. https://www.techtarget.com/searchapparchitecture/definition/interoperability.

74 Merriam-Webster. "Static Definition & Meaning." Accessed September 27, 2022. https://www.merriam-webster.com/dictionary/static.

75 Merriam-Webster. "Dynamic Definition & Meaning." Accessed September 27, 2022. https://www.merriam-webster.com/dictionary/dynamic.

76 Merriam-Webster. "Interactive Definition & Meaning." Accessed September 27, 2022. https://www.merriam-webster.com/dictionary/interactive.

77 TheStreet Staff. "What Was the Dot-Com Bubble & Why Did It Burst?" TheStreet. May 31, 2022. https://www.thestreet.com/dictionary/d/dot-com-bubble-and-burst.

78 Brian McCullough. "A revealing look at the dot-com bubble—and how it shapes our lives today." TED. December 4, 2018. https://ideas.ted.com/an-eye-opening-look-at-the-dot-com-bubble-of-2000-and-how-it-shapes-our-lives-today/.

79 Moaffak Ahmed. "Anatomy of a Crash: The dot-com bubble." Cooler Future. April 1, 2020. https://www.coolerfuture.com/blog/anatomy-of-a-crash-dot-com-bubble.

80 CFI Team. "Dotcom Bubble—Overview, Characteristics, Causes." CFI. January 21, 2022. https://corporatefinanceinstitute.com/resources/knowledge/trading-investing/dotcom-bubble/.

81 Sean A. Hays. "Transhumanism | Definition, Origins, Characteristics, & Facts." Britannica. Accessed September 27, 2022. https://www.britannica.com/topic/transhumanism.

82 Michelle Z. Donahue. "How a Color-Blind Artist Became the World's First Cyborg." National Geographic. April 3, 2017. https://www.nationalgeographic.com/science/article/worlds-first-cyborg-human-evolution-science.

83 Gwyn D'Mello. "Meet Neil Harbisson, The World's 1st True Cyborg With An Antenna Sticking Out Of His Head." India Times. February 22, 2018. https://www.indiatimes.com/technology/science-and-future/meet-neil-harbisson-the-world-s-1st-true-cyborg-with-an-antenna-sticking-out-of-his-head-340193.html.

84   Michelle Z. Donahue. "How a Color-Blind Artist Became the World's First Cyborg."

85   Fabian Takx. "Cyborg Neil Harbisson has an antenna in his head." De Ingenieur. November 3, 2017. https://www.deingenieur.nl/artikel/cyborg-neil-harbis-son-has-an-antenna-in-his-head.

86   Michelle Z. Donahue. "How a Color-Blind Artist Became the World's First Cyborg."

87   Fabian Takx. "Cyborg Neil Harbisson has an antenna in his head."

88   Pew Research Center. "Human Enhancement: Scientific and Ethical Dimensions of Genetic Engineering, Brain Chips and Synthetic Blood." July 26, 2016. https://www.pewresearch.org/science/2016/07/26/human-enhancement-the-scientific-and-ethical-dimensions-of-striving-for-perfection/.

89   Fabian Takx. "Cyborg Neil Harbisson has an antenna in his head."

90   CyborgNest. "Human Augmentation Technologies & Sensory Enhancements." Accessed September 27, 2022. https://www.cyborgnest.net/.

91   Victor Tangermann. "The Future is Here: Six Of Today's Most Advanced, Real-Life Cyborgs." Futurism. October 12, 2017. https://futurism.com/six-of-todays-most-advanced-real-life-cyborgs.

92   Alcor. "About." Accessed September 27, 2022. https://www.alcor.org/ about/.

93   Pew Research Center. "Human Enhancement: Scientific and Ethical Dimensions of Genetic Engineering, Brain Chips and Synthetic Blood."

94   Ibid.

95   Internet Hall of Fame. "Tim Berners-Lee." Accessed September 27, 2022. https://www.internethalloffame.org/inductees/tim-berners-lee.

96   Brian Getting. "Basic Definitions: Web 1.0, Web 2.0, Web 3.0." Practical Ecommerce. April 18, 2007. https://www.practicalecommerce.com/Basic-Definitions-Web-1-0-Web-2-0-Web-3-0.

97   Ibid.

98   Calvin Ebun-Amu. "What Is Web 3.0 and How Will It Help You?" MUO. February 3, 2021. https://www.makeuseof.com/what-is-web-3-0-and-how-will-it- help-you/.

99   Google. "Who controls the internet." Accessed September 27, 2022. https://www.google.com/search?q=who+controls+the+internet.

100 Robert Sanders. "The U.S. Government No Longer Controls the Internet." Insider. October 4, 2016. https://www.businessinsider.com/the-us-government-no-longer-controls-the-internet-2016-10.

101 Will Oremus. "How Silicon Valley became 'Big Tech.'" Slate. November 17, 2017. https://slate.com/technology/2017/11/how-silicon-valley-became-big-tech. html.

102 Adrian Shahbaz & Allie Funk. "Freedom on the Net 2021: The Global Drive to Control Big Tech." Freedom House. Accessed September 27, 2022. https://freedomhouse.org/report/freedom-net/2021/global-drive-control-big-tech.

103 Bernard Marr. "The Best Examples Of DAOs Everyone Should Know About." Forbes. May 25, 2022. https://www.forbes.com/sites/bernard-marr/2022/05/25/the-best-examples-of-daos-everyone-should-know-about/.

104 Fiona MacMillan. "VAK learning styles: what are they and what do they mean?" Engage Education. November 8, 2018. https://engage-education.com/us/blog/vak-learning-styles-what-are-they-and-what-do-they-mean/.

105 Sam Solomon. "A Brief History of Clip Art." July 16, 2018. https://solomon.io/brief-history-of-clip-art/.

106 Philip Townsend. " The internet's first viral meme is making a comeback." 13 News Now. May 20, 2022. https://www.13newsnow.com/article/news/history/ the-internets-first-viral-meme-appeared-in-1996- danvcing-baby-meme/291-6ddd45fe-0a09-4ab9-aa4e- 7e74a531b674.

107 Liz Heron. "Steve Jobs' Posts Thoughts on Flash." ABC News. April 29, 2010. https://abcnews.go.com/Technology/ apples-steve-jobs-posts-public-letter-ado- be-flash/ story?id=10508997.

108 William L. Hosch. "YouTube | History, Founders, & Facts." Britannica. August 4, 2022. https://www.britannica.com/ topic/YouTube.

109 Nina Goetzen. "US Digital Video Viewership Will Grow Faster in 2020 Than Expected." Insider. October 26, 2020. https://www.businessinsider.com/ us-digital-video-viewership-will-grow-faster-than- expected-2020-10.

110 Mimi An. "Content Trends: Preferences Emerge Along Generational Fault Lines." HubSpot. Accessed September 27, 2022. https://blog.hubspot.com/marketing/ content-trends-preferences.

111 Wyzowl. "The State of Video Marketing 2021." Accessed September 27, 2022. https://wyzowl.s3.eu-west-2. amazonaws.com/pdfs/Wyzowl-Video-Survey-2021.pdf.

112 Janko Roettgers. "How real-time technology is changing the animation industry." Protocol. Accessed September 27, 2022. https://www.protocol.com/news-letters/ entertainment/game-engines-hollywood?rebelltitem=1#rebe lltitem1.

113 Charles Borland. "THE BIRTH OF NEW HOLLYWOOD—Part 2: The Game Engine Revolution." Voltaku. January 5, 2021. https://www.voltaku.com/post/the-birth-of-new-hollywood-part-2.

114 Polygon. "Lights, camera, graphics: How Epic helps Hollywood." Accessed September 27, 2022. https://www.polygon.com/a/epic-4-0/lights-camera-graphics-how-epic-helps-hollywood.

115 Open Meta DAO. "Emergence Protocol: The Role of Game Engines in The Open Metaverse." Medium. May 2, 2022. https://medium.com/@ops_25520/the-emergence-protocol-the-role-of-game-engines-in-the-open-metaverse-e9f6fecbfed.

116 Arnold Kirimi. "Fireblocks introduces Web3 Engine with developer tools to accelerate ecosystem growth." CoinTelegraph. May 17, 2022. https://cointelegraph.com/news/fireblocks-introduces-web3-engine-with-developer-tools-to-acceler ate-ecosystem-growth.

117 Will Kenton. "S&P 500 Index: What It's for and Why It's Important in Investing." Investopedia. February 15, 2022. https://www.investopedia.com/terms/s/ sp500.asp.

118 Aran Ali. "Abstract is In: Intangible Assets Currently Make Up 90% of the S&P 500." Visual Capitalist. November 12, 2020. https://www.visualcapitalist.com/the-soaring-value-of-intangible-assets-in-the-sp-500/.

119 Dictionary.com. "Trademark Symbols ™, ®, ©, and SM—How To Use Each One." March 20, 2021. https://www.dictionary.com/e/trademark-copyright-registered-symbols/

120 Daniel Kurt. "Patents, Trademarks, and Copyrights: The Basics." Investo-pedia. May 4, 2022. https://www.investopedia.com/articles/investing/111014/patents-trademarks-and-copyrights-basics.asp.

121 Daniel Kurt. "Patents, Trademarks, and Copyrights: The Basics."

122 DocuSign. "How Digital Signatures Work." Accessed September 27, 2022. https://www.docusign.com/ how-it-works/electronic-signature/digital-signature/ digital-signature-faq.

123 Justin R. Muehlmeyer. "What are my chances of being issued a patent for my invention?" Peacock Law. Accessed October 1, 2022. https://peacocklaw.com/ what-are-my-chances-of-being-issued-a-patent-for-my-invention/.

124 iCommunity Labs. "5 advantages of smart contracts." Accessed September 27, 2022. https://icommunity.io/ en/5-advantages-of-smart-contracts/.

125 DigiSigner. "US Electronic Signature Laws and History." Accessed September 27, 2022. https:// www.digisigner.com/electronic-signature/ us-electronic-signature-laws-and-history/.

126 Ibid.

127 IBM. "What are smart contracts on blockchain?" Accessed September 27, 2022. https://www.ibm.com/topics/ smart-contracts.

128 iMIS. "Logging in with social media." Accessed September 27, 2022. https://help.imis.com/enterprise/features/ settings/contacts/logging_in_with_social_media.htm.

129 Apple. "Apple Cash." Accessed September 27, 2022. https://www.apple. com/apple-cash/.

130 Apple. "Wallet." Accessed September 27, 2022. https:// www.apple.com/ wallet/.

131 Apple. "Wallet."

132 Coinbase. "Coinbase Wallet." Accessed September 27, 2022. https://www. coinbase.com/wallet.

133 Metamask. "The crypto wallet for Dell, Web3 Dapps and NFTs." Accessed September 27, 2022. https://metamask.io/.

134 Trust Wallet. "Best Cryptocurrency Wallet." Accessed September 27, 2022. https://trustwallet.com/.

135 Exodus. "What are dApps and Web3 apps?" Accessed September 27, 2022. https://support.exodus.com/article/933-what-are-dapps.

136 Moralis. "What is a Web3 Wallet?" Accessed October 3, 2022. https://moralis.io/what-is-a-web3-wallet-web3-wallets-explained/.

137 Wikipedia. "Minority Report (film)." Accessed September 27, 2022. https://en.wikipedia.org/wiki/Minority_Report_(film).

138 Nick Wingfield & Mike Isaac. "Pokémon Go Brings Augmented Reality to a Mass Audience." The New York Times. July 11, 2016. https://www.nytimes.com/2016/07/12/technology/pokemon-go-brings-augmented-reality-to-a-mass-audience.html

139 PTC. "What is Augmented Reality?" Accessed September 27, 2022. https:// www.ptc.com/en/technologies/augmented-reality.

140 Virtual Reality Society. "History Of Virtual Reality." Accessed September 27, 2022. https://www.vrs.org.uk/virtual-reality/history.html.

141 Niel Patel. "When was Augmented Reality Invented?" MakeAnAppLike. October 3, 2022. https://makeanapplike.com/when-was-augmented-reality-invented/.

142 Rebekah Carter. "Virtual Reality vs Mixed Reality—Understanding the Difference." XR Today, May 14, 2021. https://www.xrtoday.com/mixed-reality/virtual-reality-vs-mixed-reality/.

143 The Times 03 Jan 2009. "Bitcoin Genesis Block Newspaper." Accessed September 27, 2022. https://www. thetimes03jan2009.com/.

144 Daniel Phillips. "The Bitcoin Genesis Block: How It All Started." Decrypt. February 10, 2021. https://decrypt.co/ 56934/the-bitcoin-genesis-block-how-it-all-started.

145 Javatpoint. "History of Blockchain." Accessed September 27, 2022. https:// www.javatpoint.com/ history-of-blockchain.

146 Jake Frankenfield. "Merkle Tree." Investopedia. July 26, 2021. https://www.investopedia.com/terms/m/ merkle-tree.asp.

147 Robert Sheldon. "A timeline and history of blockchain technology." TechTarget. August 9, 2021. https://www. techtarget.com/whatis/feature/A-time-line-and-history-of-blockchain-technology.

148 Javatpoint. "History of Blockchain."

149 Shobhit Seth. "Public, Private, Permissioned Blockchains Compared." Investopedia. July 28, 2022. https://www.investopedia.com/news/ public-private-permissioned-blockchains-compared/.

150 Gluttony777 (@gluttony777). "Create simple Blockchain using Python." GeeksforGeeks. June 3, 2022. https://www.geeksforgeeks.org/create-simple-blockchain-using-python/.

151 Webb Wright. "Author Matthew Ball Says 'the Nature Of The Metaverse All Depends On Who Pioneers It.'" The Drum. August 4, 2022. https://www.the-drum.com/ news/2022/08/04/author-matthew-ball-says-the-nature-the-metaverse-will-depend-who-pioneers-it.

152 Jon Radoff. "Metaverse Interoperability, Part 1: Challenges." Medium. January 24, 2022.

https://medium.com/building-the-metaverse/metaverse-interoperability-part-1-challenges-716455ca439e.

153 Jenifer Goodwin. "Older Folks Watch More TV, Get Less Out of It." Health Day. June 7, 2022. https://consumer.healthday.com/senior-citizen-information-31/misc-aging-news-10/older-folks-watch-more-tv-get-less-out-of-it-640678.html.

ABOUT KARY OBERBRUNNER

KARY OBERBRUNNER is a Wall Street Journal and USA Today bestselling author of eleven books. As CEO of Igniting Souls and Blockchain Life, he helps authors, entrepreneurs, and influencers publish and protect their Intellectual Property and turn it into 18 streams of income. An award-winning novelist, screenwriter, and inventor, he's been featured in Entrepreneur, CBS, Fox News, Yahoo, and many other major media outlets.

As a young man, he suffered from severe stuttering, depression, and self-injury. Today a transformed man, Kary ignites souls. He speaks internationally on a variety of topics including leadership, personal growth, human performance, blockchain technology, and entrepreneurship. As a futurist, he often consults on marketing, branding, Intellectual Property, and Web3.

He has several earned degrees, including a Bachelor of Arts, Masters in Divinity, and Doctorate in Transformational Leadership. He lives in Ohio with his family.

ABOUT LEE RICHTER

Award-winning CEO, Marketing Expert, Innovator and Global Leader, Lee Richter, is recognized for many years as one of San Francisco's Top 100 Women Business Leaders, Top 100 Fastest Growing Businesses … and in 2022, she was named one of the Top 100 Innovators in the San Francisco Bay Area by the San Francisco Business Times.

Expanding on her successful entrepreneurial journey, Lee utilizes her superpower in public relations to connect the business world with the future of business and marketing.

She inspires entrepreneurs and business owners to realize the importance of NFTs and blockchain and empowers them to develop and implement a strategy in their company. Lee teaches leaders globally to incorporate NFTs in their business as a tactic to achieve financial and professional success in the current marketplace. In addition, she is a best-selling co-author of "Blockchain Life" and is exploring and identifying ways the blockchain is changing how we conduct business in the future.

Most importantly, Lee is a loving and devoted wife and mother. With Lee's help, her daughter Abbey became a best-selling author... at the age of 9, and her husband is recognized as a global thought leader in the veterinary industry for his expertise in holistic health for pets and effective integrative medicine. Lee and her family follow their passion as they love to travel and explore the world together while meeting interesting people and global leaders along the way!

Enjoy Kary's Other Books

AVAILABLE WHEREVER BOOKS ARE SOLD

INTERESTED IN FINDING OUT MORE ABOUT NFTS?

Lee Richter is dedicated to educating and training global leaders in all aspects of the NFT space.

KEYNOTE SPEAKER

START THE CONVERSATION TODAY

GOASKLEE.COM

NFTS 101

Where to Begin, How to Master Them, and Why You Need Them...

Learn the fundamentals of NFT technology from what they are and how they work to important NFT marketplaces and advanced tips to get you ahead in this space.

Learn More At:
nftswithlee.com

INTELLECTUAL PROPERTY
PROTECTION FOR
THE WEB3 WORLD.

EasyIP.Today

WHAT'S YOUR
WQ?

Prepare for the biggest revolution in human history.

Determine your Web Quotient™

TheBlockchainLife.io

WRITE AND PUBLISH YOUR BOOK

Join Kary in Virtual Reality
A FUN WAY TO ACHIEVE YOUR DREAM

RETREATVR.IO/KARY

BLOCKCHAIN
VERIFIED IP™

Powered by Easy IP™

Made in the USA
Las Vegas, NV
29 March 2023

69843105R00103